Ducks

by Harry M. Lamon and Rob R. Slocum

PREFACE

Of all lines of poultry keeping, duck raising is unique in that it lends itself to the greatest degree of specialization and intensification along lines which are purely commercial. On a comparatively small area thousands of ducklings can be reared and marketed yearly. The call for information concerning the methods used by these commercial duck raisers has been considerable, and since such information is not available in complete concise form the present book has been prepared partly to furnish just this information.

The methods used by successful Long Island duck raisers differ widely in some particulars and since in the space at command, it has been impossible to describe all the methods used, the plan has been adopted of detailing in the main the methods of one successful grower. This it is believed will prove to be more helpful and less confusing than to attempt to give the method of several different men.

Much space has been given to the operations of the commercial duck raisers but the fact is recognized that the great bulk of the ducks entering into the trade of the country is the product of small flocks kept on general farms. For this reason a chapter has been added dealing with duck raising on the farm, and attention is here called to the fact that most of the information given under commercial duck raising can be readily adapted to use in connection with the farm flock.

Detailed, complete information on goose raising is even more fragmentary than is the case with ducks. Yet there is a fine opportunity to rear a few geese at a profit on many farms, and the need and call for information is quite general. It is for this reason that a section of this book has been devoted to goose raising and in that section all the good reliable information available on the subject is given. The special attention of the women of the farm is directed to the opportunity which goose raising offers to make a good profit on a small side line with the minimum of initial investment and of labor.

The greatest care has been taken to make the information on both duck and goose raising as complete and clear as possible. However, the authors appreciate the unlimited value of good illustrations in making clear methods and operations which are more difficult to grasp from a word description, and have therefore assembled a set of illustrations for this book, the completeness and excellence of which have never before been approached in any book on the subject. The illustrations alone are an education.

In preparing and presenting this book to the public, the authors take pleasure in acknowledging their deep indebtedness to the following persons for help and information furnished:

Roy E. Pardee John C. Kriner Charles McClave Stanley Mason Dr. Balliet William Minnich George W. Hackett Dawson Brothers

Particular acknowledgment is due Robert A. Tuttle for the manner in which he threw open his duck plant to the authors and for the most generous amount of time which he gave in furnishing information.

Special acknowledgment is likewise due Alfred R. Lee, Poultryman, U. S. Department of Agriculture, for information secured from his Farmers' Bulletins on duck raising and goose raising.

TABLE OF CONTENTS

Apparatus--Pens--Equipment of the Pens--Grading and Sorting the Ducklings--Cleaning and Bedding the Pens--Ventilation--Other Types of Brooder Houses--Length of Time in Brooder House No. 1--Brooder House No. 2--Brooder House No. 3--Yard Accommodations for Ducklings--Shade--Feeding--Lights for Ducklings--Pounds of Feed to Produce a Pound of Market Duck--Water for Young Ducks--Age and Weight when Ready for Market--Cripples--Cleaning the Yards--Critical Period with Young Ducks--Disease Prevention--Gapes or Pneumonia--Fits--Diarrhoea--Lameness--Sore Eyes--Feather Eating or Quilling--Rats--Cooperative Feed Association.

DUCKS

PART I

Chapter I

Present Extent of the Industry

Duck raising while representing an industry of considerable value to the United States when considered from a national standpoint, is one of the minor branches of the poultry industry. According to the 1920 census there were 2,817,624 ducks in the United States with a valuation of $3,373,966. As compared with this the census for 1910 shows a slightly greater number of ducks, 2,906,525, but their value was considerably less being only $1,567,164. In the ten years between the census of 1900 and that of 1910 there was a decrease in the number of ducks of nearly 40%.

According to the 1920 census the more important duck raising states arranged in their order of importance were Iowa, Illinois, Pennsylvania, New York, Missouri, Minnesota, Tennessee, Ohio, South Dakota, Indiana, Nebraska and Kentucky. The number reported for Iowa was 235,249 and for Kentucky 99,577. New England, the North Atlantic, the East North Central, the West North Central, the Mountain and the Pacific states showed an increase, while the South Atlantic, East South Central and West South Central states showed a decrease. In spite of the existence of quite a number of large commercial duck farms, the great bulk of ducks produced are those which come from the general farms where only small flocks are kept. Yet only a small proportion of farms have ducks on them. The comparatively small number of ducks is distributed over practically the entire United States, being more common in some sections than others, particularly along the Atlantic Coast and along the Pacific Coast, with fairly numerous flocks on the farms of the Middle West.

Different Types of Duck Raising. The conditions under which ducks are kept and the purpose for which they are kept fall under four heads: First, commercial duck raising for the production of duck meat; second, duck raising as a by-product of the general farm; third, duck raising for egg production; fourth, duck breeding for pleasure, exhibition or the sale of breeding stock.

Opportunities for Duck Raising. Undoubtedly the greatest opportunity for profitable duck growing lies under the first of these heads, namely, commercial duck raising. Where the conditions of climate, soil and land are favorable and where the location is good with respect to market there exists an excellent opportunity for one skilled in duck growing to engage in that business in an intensive manner for the purpose of putting on the market spring or green ducklings. Where these are in demand they bring a good price and since the output per farm is large they pay a good return even with a small margin of profit per pound.

The second greatest opportunity undoubtedly consists of duck raising as a by-product of the general farm. Where conditions are suitable, that is to say, where there is a considerable amount of pasture land easily accessible, and particularly where there is a stream or pond to which the ducks can have access, a small flock of ducks, say 10 or 12 females, can be kept to excellent advantage on the farm. The cost of maintaining them will not be great and they will not only provide a most acceptable variety in the form of duck meat and duck eggs for the farmers' table but they will also produce a surplus which can be sold at a profit. It must be remembered, however, that where only a small flock is kept it is generally impracticable for the farmer to give his ducks the attention necessary to cater to the market for green ducklings. As a result he usually keeps them until fall and sells them on the market at a considerably lower price than is obtained by the commercial duck grower.

There also exists an opportunity which has not been developed to any great extent to keep some one of the egg producing breeds of ducks such as the Indian Runner for the primary purpose of egg production. A few ventures of this sort seem to have been successful but it must be remembered that the market for duck eggs is not nearly so broad as that for hens' eggs and that in some quarters there exists considerable prejudice against duck eggs for table consumption. Before engaging in duck raising primarily for the production of market eggs it would therefore be necessary to investigate and consider carefully the market conditions in the neighborhood so as to know whether the eggs could be marketed to advantage. While the Runner ducks are prolific layers there is no advantage in keeping them in preference to fowls as egg producers. The eggs are larger in size but it takes more feed to produce them, while they cannot as a rule be disposed of at much if any higher price than can be secured for hens' eggs. For baking purposes duck eggs can be readily sold on account of their larger size.

There is always an opportunity to produce fine stock of any kind, whether it be ducks, chickens, turkeys or geese. Ducks are not exhibited to the same extent as are chickens and the competition in the shows is not as a rule so keen. Nevertheless many persons are interested in producing and exhibiting good stock and there exists a very definite market for birds of quality.

There is also a probability that a good business could be worked up by one who would pay special attention to producing a strain of ducks of early maturity, large size and good vigor in order to supply breeding drakes to many of the commercial duck farms. These farms usually secure drakes for breeding from sources outside their own flocks each year but the usual practice is to exchange drakes with some other commercial grower. While very good birds are to be found on these duck farms there is no greater opportunity to engage in any systematic breeding, the selection of the breeding stock being of rather a hurried nature during certain seasons of the year when the ducks are being marketed. Moreover, the long continued custom of exchanging drakes with the neighboring farmers has in most cases led to the blood being so largely confined within one circle that no great percentage of new blood is obtained by these exchanges. Of course, the opportunity along breeding lines for this purpose is limited to the Pekin duck as this is the breed which is kept upon all the large commercial duck farms in the United States.

Prices for Breeding Stock. Duck breeders who make a specialty of selling breeding stock or eggs for hatching find a steady and quite a wide demand for their stock. The eggs are usually sold in sittings of 11 and bring a price of from $3 to $5 per sitting depending on the quality of the stock. The prices received for the birds themselves depend of course upon their quality and may run anywhere from about $5 to $25 per bird.

Ducks for Ornamental Purposes. On estates or in parks where natural or artificial ponds are included in the grounds, waterfowl are often kept for ornamental purposes. Any breeds may be used, and often the gay colored Wood Duck and Mandarin, or some one of the small breeds such as the Calls, Black East Indian or the Mallards are kept for this purpose. It is said that these small ducks will absolutely destroy the mosquito larvae in any such ponds or lakes.

CHAPTER II

Breeds and Varieties--How to Mate to Produce Exhibition Specimens--
Preparing Ducks for the Show--Catching and Handling

Breeds of Ducks. There are 11 standard breeds of ducks. All of these breeds
with the exception of the Call, Muscovy and Runner consist of a single variety.
The Call is divided into two varieties, the Gray and the White; the Muscovy
consists of two varieties, the Colored and the White; and the Runner consists
of three varieties, the Fawn and White, the White and the Penciled.

Duck breeders, of course, whether raising the birds for fancy or for profit,
keep one of the standard breads or varieties. Frequently, also, the farm flocks
consist of standardbred ducks but on many farms, probably a great majority,
the flock consists of the common or so-called "puddle" duck. In certain parts
of the South there is a duck known as the "mule duck" which is a cross
between the Muscovy and the common duck. This is a duck of good market
quality but will not breed from which characteristic it gets its name. Most of
the common or "puddle" ducks which are found on farms are of rather small
size, are indifferent as layers, and do not make a desirable type of market duck.
They have arisen simply from the crossing of standard breeds with resultant
carelessness and indifference in breeding. Because of the care with which they
have been selected and bred for definite purposes, the standard breeds are
decidedly superior to the common "puddle" ducks and should by all means be
kept in preference since they will yield better results and greater profits.

In addition to the standard breeds and varieties flocks of Mallards are also
kept to a limited extent. The Mallard is a common small wild duck which has
lent itself readily to domestication and which thrives with proper care under
confined conditions. In weight, the drakes will run from 2?pounds to 3 pounds
or even a little larger. The ducks average about 2?pounds with a variation of
from 1 pound 12 ounces to 2 pounds 8 ounces. By selecting the large eggs for
hatching and by liberal feeding, it is easy to increase the size of Mallards to
such an extent that they resemble small Rouens rather than wild Mallards. The
plumage of the Mallard is very similar to that of the Rouen but of a lighter
shade. Another small wild duck known as the Wood or Carolina duck, which

is a native of North America, has been domesticated and on account of the great beauty of its plumage is usually to be found wherever ornamental waterfowl are kept. The Mandarin duck is a small duck of about the same size as the Wood duck, is of beautiful plumage and like the Wood duck is generally kept for ornamental purposes. This duck is said to be a native of China.

Classification of Breeds

So far as the standard breeds and varieties are concerned they may be divided into three classes according to the purpose for which they are kept and for which they are best suited. First is the meat class which consists of the Pekin, Aylesbury, Muscovy, Rouen, Buff, Cayuga and Blue Swedish. These breeds could well be termed general purpose ducks for they are quite good layers in addition to producing excellent table carcasses and are therefore well suited for general farm use. They are, however, kept more particularly for meat production.

The second class is known as the egg class and consists of the three varieties of the Runner Duck, formerly known as the Indian Runner. The Runner Duck is much smaller in size than the birds of the meat class, is longer in leg and more active, and is not so well suited for the production of table ducks but is a very prolific layer. With proper feeding and management the Runner ducks will compare favorably with hens as egg producers.

The third class is known as the ornamental class and is composed of the ducks which are kept and bred principally for ornamental purposes. This class consists of the Call duck with its two varieties, the Black East India duck and the Crested White duck. Both the Call and East India ducks are small in size being really the bantams of the duck family. While they make good table birds, their small size handicaps them as commercial meat fowl. The Crested White duck is of larger size, possesses a crest and is bred mainly as an ornamental fowl.

Marking the Ducks. The duck raiser who is breeding his ducks for exhibition quality has need for knowledge of the breeding of the birds he may contemplate using in his matings. In order that this information may be available, the young ducks as they are hatched can be marked by toe punching them on the webs of their feet in the same manner that baby chicks are toe punched. A different set or combination of marks is used for each mating so that the breeding of the different ducks can be distinguished. Mature ducks can, if desired, be leg banded in order to furnish a distinguishing mark.

Nomenclature

Before taking up a description of the matings of the different standard breeds and varieties it is well to indicate the common nomenclature which is used in connection with these fowls and which differs from that used for chickens. The male duck is called drake, the female duck is termed duck, and the young duck of either sex is termed duckling. In giving the standard weights for the different breeds of ducks, weights are given for adult ducks and adult drakes, and for young ducks and young drakes. By adult duck or drake is meant a bird which is over one year old. By young duck or drake is meant a bird which is less than one year old. The horny mouth parts of the duck instead of being termed beak as in chickens are called bill, and the separate division of the upper bill at its extremity is termed the bean. Ducks do not show any comb or wattles as in chickens. In England use is made of the terms ducklet and drakerel. Ducklet is used to signify a female during her first laying season just as the word pullet is used in contrast to hen. Drakerel is used to signify a young drake as contrasted with an older drake just as the word cockerel is used in comparison to cock in chickens.

Distinguishing the Sex. The sex of mature ducks can be readily told by their voices and also by a difference in the feathering. The duck gives voice to a coarse, harsh sound which is the characteristic "quack" usually thought of in connection with this class of fowl. The drake on the other hand utters a cry which is not nearly so loud or harsh but which is more of a hissing sound. Distinction of sex by this means can be made after the ducklings are from 4 to 6 weeks old. Before this age, both sexes make the same peeping noise.

Mature drakes are also distinguished from the ducks by the presence of two sex feathers at the base of the tail. These are short feathers which curl or curve upward and forward toward the body of the bird. In ducks these feathers are absent.

Size

An idea of the size of the different standard breeds can best be obtained by giving the standard weights. They are as follows:--

Adult Drake. Adult Duck. Young Drake. Young Duck. Pekin 9 8 8 7 Aylesbury 9 8 8 7 Rouen 9 8 8 7 Cayuga 8 7 7 6 Muscovy 10 7 8 6 Blue Swedish 8 7 6?5?Crested White 7 6 6 5 Buff 8 7 7 6 Runner 4?4 4 3?

There are no standard weights for the Call duck and for the Black East India duck but these are all small in size, being really bantam ducks. The drakes will weigh from 2?to 3 pounds and the ducks from 2 to 2?pounds.

Popularity of Breeds

In the meat class by far the most popular duck in this country is the Pekin. It is the breed which is used exclusively on the large commercial duck farms. Next to the Pekin in this class probably comes the Muscovy which is quite commonly kept in some sections of the country, particularly in the South. The Aylesbury duck has never proved to be very popular in the United States perhaps due to its white bill and skin, although it is the popular market duck of England. The other breeds included in the meat class are kept more or less commonly but do not approach in popularity either the Pekin or the Muscovy. Any of the breeds in this class will prove to be satisfactory for a farm flock, although the Colored breeds and varieties are at a disadvantage when dressed due to their dark pin feathers.

In the egg class there is included only the Indian Runner and this of course is the breed which is kept wherever the production of duck eggs is the primary object. The Fawn and White is the most popular variety of this breed.

In the ornamental class there is no particular outstanding breed, since the ducks belonging in this class are kept very largely to satisfy the pleasure of the owner and the selection of a breed is entirely a matter of personal preference.

Egg Production

While the conditions under which ducks are kept and the care they are given will affect their egg production greatly, there are certain rather definite comparisons that can be made between the different breeds. The Pekin is a good layer and will produce from 80 to 120 eggs. The Aylesbury and the

Rouen are about alike in laying ability, neither being quite as good as the Pekin. The Cayuga is a good layer ranking with the Aylesbury and Rouen or between these and the Pekin. The Muscovy is an excellent layer being fully as prolific as the Pekin, especially if broken up when broody and not allowed to sit. The Blue Swedish is about equal to the Cayuga in laying ability. The Buff duck is an excellent layer comparing favorably with the Pekin or even with the Runner. The Runner ducks are the best layers of the duck family and if given proper care and good feed will compare favorably with hens in egg producing ability. The Crested White duck is not a particularly good layer. The Calls and the Black East India ducks will lay from 20 to 60 eggs per year, approaching the latter number if the eggs are collected as laid and the ducks are not allowed to sit which will induce some of them to continue to lay for quite a portion of the year. Extremely large ducks of any breed do not lay as well as the more medium sized birds.

Size of Duck Eggs. The eggs of the different meat breeds will run about the same in size with the exception of the Muscovy whose eggs run a little larger. Actual weights of eggs from representative flocks show Pekin, Rouen, Aylesbury and Cayuga eggs to average about 2?pounds per dozen although there is a tendency for the Rouen eggs to run somewhat larger and for Cayugas to run a little smaller. Muscovy eggs weigh about 3 pounds per dozen with selected large eggs weighing as high as 3?pounds. Eggs of the Runner duck are smaller but are considerably larger than average hens' eggs or about the size of large Minorca eggs. They weigh about 2 pounds per dozen. Eggs of the bantam breeds of ducks, the Calls and the Black East India, together with those of the Mandarin and Wood ducks will weigh from one pound to 1?pounds per dozen depending upon the size of the ducks themselves. Eggs of the Mallard duck will run from 26 to 32 ounces to the dozen. The size of eggs laid by ducks, especially the bantam breeds and the Mallard can be increased somewhat by liberal feeding. Average hens' eggs should weigh about 1?pounds per dozen.

Color of Eggs. The color of duck eggs ranges from white to a polished black. Pekin eggs run mostly white although some show a decided blue or green tint. Aylesbury eggs run quite uniformly white. The color of Rouen eggs varies from white to a dark green. The Cayuga produces very few white eggs, most of them being green or black, some being as black as though polished. Muscovy eggs run from a white to a greenish cream in color. The eggs of the

Blue Swedish and the Buff ducks usually run white. The Runner duck lays white eggs as a rule while the Crested White duck lays eggs which range in color from white to green. The eggs of the Call ducks run from white to green while the eggs of the Black East India, like the Cayuga, for the most part run from green to black.

A peculiarity in regard to the egg color is that the same female may lay eggs which are widely different in color. It is likewise true that the color of the shell is influenced to some extent by the feed. Ducks on range will lay darker colored eggs than those which are yarded. There is also a tendency for the eggs to run darker in color when laying first begins and for the eggs to lighten as laying proceeds. A peculiarity in regard to duck eggs with a dark colored shell is that a thorough washing will lighten up the shell color decidedly.

Broodiness. The Muscovy, the Call and the Black East India ducks are broody breeds. The ducks of these breeds will make their nests, hatch their eggs and are good mothers. All the other breeds are classed as non-broody breeds. Of course, a certain percentage of them will go broody and show a desire to sit but they do not make reliable sitters and mothers and are not as a rule used for this purpose.

Considerations in Making the Mating[1]

Since ducks are kept for different purposes there will of course be certain fundamental differences in the different classes in the selection of the individuals to make up the mating. Whatever the purpose, however, the first consideration in selecting the breeders must be to secure those which possess excellent vigor and general health and which meet insofar as possible the standard requirements for size. Where the Call duck and the Black East India are concerned the selection for size must be for smallness since that is a characteristic greatly desired. In the other breeds the selection for size must be to see that they come up to the standard weights for the particular breed in question. As in other classes of fowls the condition and cleanliness of the plumage and the general appearance and actions of the birds are good indications of their health and thriftiness. A bright eye is likewise a valuable indication of good health while a watery eye is usually a sign of weakness. It is necessary to guard against birds which show any tendency toward crooked or roach back, hump back, crooked tails, or twisted wings. Since all breeds of ducks should have clean or unfeathered legs it is likewise necessary to guard against any breeders which show down on the shanks or between the toes as this sometimes occurs.

[Footnote 1: For a more detailed discussion of the principles of breeding as applied to chickens and which is equally applicable to ducks, the reader is referred to "The Mating and Breeding of Poultry" by Harry M. Lamon and Rob R. Slocum, published by the Orange Judd Publishing Company, New York City.]

In selecting the mating for any one of the meat breeds use birds which have good length, width and depth of body so that they will have plenty of meat carrying capacity. For breeders of market ducks, birds which are active, well matured and which are not extreme in size for the breed are preferable as the fertility is likely to run better than with the extremely large birds. Where birds are bred for exhibition purposes, it frequently happens that it is desirable to use large breeders and to hold them for breeding purposes as long as they are in good breeding condition. Where this is the case it becomes necessary to mate a smaller number of females to a drake than would be the case with smaller and younger breeders. Where old birds are used as breeders better results will be secured by mating old ducks to a young drake or vice versa than by mating together old birds of both sexes. While ducks of any of the meat breeds are kept primarily for meat production, it is essential that the egg production be good throughout the breeding season in order to raise as many ducklings and secure as great a profit as possible. Selection of the females as breeders should be made therefore on the basis of good egg production as well as good meat type if the conditions under which the ducks are kept are such as to make it possible to check this in any manner.

In selecting the mating in the Runner breed it is necessary to keep in mind that the general type of body is quite different from that of the meat breeds, being much slimmer and much more upright in body carriage. For this mating select thrifty, healthy birds and those which are active. Some breeders trapnest their Runner ducks or have some other means of checking up the better layers. As in chickens, it is of course desirable to use these better layers as breeders since the purpose in keeping this kind of duck is primarily egg production.

In selecting the mating in the Call and East India breeds it is necessary to use the smaller ducks since the object here is to keep the size small. In addition, with these breeds or with any other breeds kept and bred primarily for fancy or exhibition purposes, it is necessary to conform just as closely as possible to the standard requirements[2] both insofar as size and type are concerned, and also with respect to color.

[Footnote 2: For a complete and official description and list of disqualifications of the standard breeds and varieties of ducks, the reader is referred to the American Standard of Perfection published by the American Poultry Association, and obtained by Orange Judd Publishing Company, New York, N. Y.]

Breeds of Ducks

The Pekin. While this variety wants to be of good size and to have length, breadth and depth of body it is somewhat more upstanding than some of the other meat breeds, showing a definite slope of body downward from shoulders to tail. The back line of the Pekin should show a slight concavity from the shoulders to the tail and the upper line of the bill is likewise slightly concave between the point where it joins the head and its extremity. The shoulders should be broad and any tendency toward narrowness at this point must be avoided. While a good depth of keel is desired, the standard does not call for so deep a keel as in the Aylesbury. As a matter of fact, however, the winning specimens as seen in the shows are not as a rule as erect in carriage as called for by the standard illustration, there being a tendency to get them almost if not quite as deep in keel as the Aylesbury. In fact, some breeders seem to strive for a low down keel approaching a condition where they are nearly as low in front as behind but this is not desirable Pekin type.

Sometimes a drake will show a rough neck, that is, the feathers on the back of the neck will be crossed or folded over showing a tendency to curl. These birds should be avoided as breeders since there is a tendency for them to produce ducks having a crest. Sometimes a green or a greenish spotted bill will be encountered. Since the bill should be a clear yellow, breeders showing this defect should be avoided particularly as they are likely to produce birds having greenish or olive colored legs. The shanks and toes should be a clear deep orange. Black sometimes occurs in the bean. This may occur in birds of either sex but is more common in the ducks than in the drakes. In the drake black in the bean disqualifies but while it is undesirable and a serious defect in the duck it does not disqualify. The color of the plumage is white or creamy white throughout. Creaminess in this variety is not a serious defect as it is in white chickens. The use, however, of yellow corn and of foods very rich in oil tends to increase the creaminess of the plumage and should not be used to excess for birds which are to be exhibited.

The Aylesbury. This breed is particularly noted for its deep keel. It differs from the Pekin in type in that it is more nearly level in body. There is a decided tendency for the Aylesbury to run too short in body which has probably come about by extreme selection for deep keel. It is well, therefore, in making the mating to select breeders with good length of body. Since the deep full breast and keel is characteristic of this breed it is necessary to avoid breeders which show any tendency toward a flat breast. As in the case of the Pekins avoid any birds which have green or olive colored bills. The back line of the Aylesbury should be straight, showing no tendency toward a slight concavity as in the Pekin. Birds showing this shape back should be avoided. As in the Pekin black on the bill or bean of the drake will disqualify and in the duck is a serious defect. The color of plumage should be white throughout and should show no tendency toward creaminess. The bill in this breed is flesh colored instead of yellow as in the Pekin. The Aylesbury is not quite as nervous a breed as the Pekin.

The Rouen. The Rouen duck is a parti-colored breed and is therefore much more difficult to secure in perfection of color and marking than is the case with the white breeds. Moreover, the dark pin feathers make the ducks more difficult to dress than in white breeds. In type these birds are very level in body and are massive, carrying a great deal of meat. Avoid birds showing a lack of length of body or depth of keel or which are too flat in breast. The back of the Rouen should have a slightly convex or arched shape from neck to tail and it is necessary to guard against birds which have a flat or a concave back. The body of the Rouen should be carried practically horizontal. The upper line of the bill should be slightly dished or concave. The white ring about the neck of the drake is an important part of the marking. This should not be too wide but should run about a quarter of an inch in width. It should be as distinct and clean cut as possible but should not quite come together in the rear. Any approach to a ring in the female is a disqualification. White in the primary or secondary wing feathers is a serious defect since it constitutes a disqualification. It must therefore be carefully avoided. White feathers in the fluff of the drake is another color defect which must be guarded against.

Breast of Drake. The farther the claret color on the breast of the drake extends down the better will be the females secured from the mating. Drakes which are deficient in the amount of claret on the breast should therefore be thrown out as breeders. A purple rump in drakes must be avoided as must black feathers over the rump as they tend to keep up too dark a body color in the female. On the other hand too bright or light a color in the male or exhibition female will produce females which are too light in color. Drakes with light olive colored bills must be avoided as these will have a tendency to produce offspring which show too much yellow in the females' bills, and clear yellow bills constitute a disqualification. In the females solid yellow bills, fawn colored breasts and absence of penciling must be avoided. Females which are dark or nearly black over the rump are good breeders as they tend to keep up the ground color of the body and tail.

The Rouen shows some tendency to fade in color. This is evidenced first on the tips of the wings. The fading will also show in the fluff of drakes. The drakes of this breed and likewise of the Gray Call and the Mallard show a peculiar behavior with respect to the color of their plumage. About June 1 the drakes moult, losing their characteristic male adult plumage and the new plumage is practically that of the female. This female plumage is retained until about October when they gradually regain their normal winter male plumage. Young Rouens of both sexes have female plumage until the last moult which occurs at about four or five months of age, when the drakes assume the adult male plumage. The sex of the young Rouens can, however, be told by the difference in the color of the bills.

The Cayuga. The Cayuga is much like the other breeds of the meat class in general type or shape of body showing good length, breadth and depth. It is a very solid duck and weighs heavier than it looks. The body carriage is slightly more upright than the Rouen but not so much so as the Pekin. The back line should be straight and any tendency toward an arched back must be avoided. It is slightly smaller than the Pekin, Aylesbury and Rouen, averaging about a pound less.

In making the mating, size is important and breeders should be selected which are up to standard weights if possible. While this breed is not kept very widely at the present time, nevertheless it is an excellent market duck, dressing out into a very plump yellow carcass in spite of its black plumage which is a disadvantage in dressing. The color should be a lustrous greenish black throughout, being somewhat brighter in the drake than in the duck. The duck is more likely to show a brownish cast of plumage, particularly as she grows older. It is hard to hold good black color with age. Moreover, white or gray is apt to occur in the breast of females. With age also a little white sometimes develops on the back of the neck, around the eyes and underneath the neck at the base of the bill. The white which occurs in breast is more likely to come in ducks and is not commonly found in the drakes. In the drakes on the other hand, there is a tendency for the white to come on the throat under the bill.

Drakes as a rule run truer in color and hold their color better than do the ducks. Where the white mottling occurs in plumage with age one need not hesitate to breed from these birds if they were of good black color as young birds. The drakes of the best color do not as a rule fade or become mottled to any great extent with age. It is necessary to guard against birds as breeders which have a rusty brown lacing on the breast and under the wings, also those which have a wing-bow laced with brown. There is a tendency for the bill of drakes, which should be black, to be too light or olive in color and this tendency increases with age. Drakes with bills of this color should be avoided as breeders. When Cayugas are first hatched the baby ducks all show a white breast.

The Call. The Call ducks are the bantams of the duck race. There is always a tendency for them to grow too large and this is especially true when they have an opportunity to eat all they want as for example when they are fed with the larger ducks. They should not be fed too liberally and should be given wheat or some other solid grain rather than any mash. If there is a good pond of water to which the Call ducks can have access they do not need to be fed much of anything.

In breeding, the smallest individuals which are suitable in other respects for breeders, should be selected in order to keep down the size and offset the tendency to breed larger in successive generations. In type the Calls are practically miniature Pekins except that they should have a very short, rather broad head and bill. The broad flat and short bill and the round short head give the head an appearance which is often described by the term "button headed". In this breed avoid birds which show arched backs. The body should have what is known as a flatiron shape, that is, should be broad at the shoulders and taper toward the tail. Too deep keels and narrow shoulders should be avoided as should also too long bills. Call ducks, together with East Indias and Mallards should have their wings clipped or be pinioned, that is, have the first joint of one wing cut off, to prevent them from flying away.

The Gray Call. The plumage of the Gray Call is practically that of the Rouen although they are not quite as good in color as a breed. There is more of a tendency for some of the birds to run to dark and others, especially the males, to run too light in color. While they are likely to be well penciled the shade of color is apt to be wrong. White in the flights and under the wings must be guarded against as must also absence of ribbon or wing bar in females. The color of the plumage is likely to fade with age but after the birds moult and secure their new plumage, the color is usually higher again. In general the same color characteristics hold true as with the Rouen and the same defects must be guarded against.

The White Call. This variety is, both in type and color, practically a miniature Pekin except for the short, rather broad head and bill. They breed very true in color and should be free from creaminess. The same general defects must be watched for and avoided as in the Pekin.

The Black East India. This is a black breed which is small in size being a bantam duck like the Call. As a matter of fact it is a miniature Cayuga. The color should be black throughout and the same color characteristics hold true as in the case of the Cayuga. The same color defects must therefore be guarded against, the worst one being white in the breast of females especially. Avoid breeding from a drake with a black bill as in this respect the breed differs from the Cayuga since the bill of the duck should be black but that of the drake should be very dark green. Purple barring must be carefully selected against.

The Muscovy. This breed differs in certain respects very markedly from the other standard breeds of ducks. They are long and broad in body which is carried in a horizontal position but are not so deep in keel as the Pekin, Aylesbury or Rouen. The longest bodied young ducks will make the largest individuals. The head should have feathers on the top which can be elevated at will to form a crest. Guard against breeders having smooth heads, or in other words, lacking a crest. The face is covered with corrugations or caruncles and should be red in color. At the base of the upper bill there is a sort of knob-like formation in the drake which serves as one of the distinguishing characteristics between the duck and drake of this breed. The more prominent the knob and the more wrinkled or corrugated the face the better is the specimen in this respect. The wings are long and strong and these birds fly very well. They will also climb fences. The drakes are quite pugnacious and fight one another badly at times. They are especially pugnacious when they have young.

This breed of ducks will often roost on roosts like chickens or in the trees or on the barn. They do not quack like other ducks and unlike other domesticated breeds which moult two or three times a year, they moult only once, taking longer to do so, usually about 90 days, although the female may complete her moult a little sooner. The period of incubation for Muscovy eggs is longer, being from 33 to 35 days as compared to 28 days for other breeds. In size the male and female differ considerably as will be seen from the standard weights given (See Page 14), the male being considerably larger. These ducks lay well, the fertility runs good, the eggs hatch well, and the little ducks are hardy and easily raised. They are a broody breed. The ducks will make their nests and hatch out their eggs if allowed to do so and are excellent mothers. Sometimes they will fly up and make their nests in a hollow tree. A Muscovy duck can cover properly about 20 eggs. In spite of the fact that they fly well they are easily domesticated. It takes about two years for the males of this breed to fully mature although the ducks get their full size when one year of age. The Muscovy is perhaps the best general purpose breed for a farm flock.

The extent and intensity of the red of the face increases up to maturity and the redder the face the better. The plumage of the Muscovy is not as downy or oily as other breeds, the feathers being harder. For this reason the birds are more apt to become water soaked and to drown as a result when they have not been accustomed to water in which to swim. This is especially true of the drakes on account of their large size and long wing feathers. Muscovy ducks dress well, having a rich yellow skin, and therefore make a good market duck, although the difference in size of the duck and drake and the dark pin feathers of the Colored variety are disadvantages from a market standpoint. Select against breeders which run small in size as there is more or less of a tendency for this breed to decrease in size. The Muscovy is long lived, specimens having been known to breed until they were eight or ten years of age.

The Colored Muscovy. Although the standard calls for more or less white in different sections of this variety, as a matter of fact breeders desire to get the birds as dark as possible except for a very small patch of white on the breast and a small patch of white on the center of the wing. Indeed, birds without the white on the breast and with very little on the wing are valuable breeders since there is a tendency for too much white to occur in the plumage. Occasionally all black birds occur and these can be used to advantage in breeding when there is a tendency toward too much white in plumage. Plumage more than half white is a disqualification. The dark plumage birds such as are wanted are very likely to show considerable black or gypsy color in the face which should be a good red. This must be selected against insofar as possible. The nearly black or the darkest birds are quite likely to show some white or grizzling on the head. Grizzled or brownish penciled feathers sometimes occur in various parts of the plumage and must of course be guarded against as the markings should be distinctly black and white. The baby ducks of this variety are quite apt to show considerable white although the best of them come yellowish black. This variety tends to run a little larger in size than the white variety although the standard weights are the same for both. Dun or chocolate colored ducks sometimes come from Colored Muscovies while Blue Muscovies can be produced by crossing the Colored and the white varieties.

The White Muscovy. This variety should have pure white plumage throughout. Young Muscovies of both sexes often have a patch of black on top of the head up to the time they moult at maturity. Since black disqualifies it is impossible to show young ducks in this condition but these black feathers usually come in white after the moult and such birds need not therefore be discarded as breeders. When it is desired to show young White Muscovies which have black on the head it is customary to pluck these black feathers a sufficient time before the show so that the white feathers which come in their place will have time to grow out. There is little or no trouble with black or gypsy face in this variety.

The Blue Swedish. In type and size this breed is about the same as the Cayuga although perhaps slightly more upstanding. In selecting the mating it is important to use birds which are close to standard weight as there is somewhat of a tendency for the size to be too small. As its name indicates the color is largely blue except for a white heart-shaped patch or bib which should be present on the breast. Sometimes this white extends along the underside of the body from the under-bill almost to the vent. Such birds are undesirable as breeders since they show too much white. On the other hand birds lacking a prominent white bib must also be avoided. Two of the flight feathers should be white and birds lacking these must be avoided. Guard against any red, gray or black in any part of the plumage. Sometimes, however, birds having more or less black throughout the plumage are used as breeders for the purpose of strengthening the blue color. Avoid any tendency toward a ribbon on the wing-bow and also birds that are too light, ashy or washed out in the blue color.

Sometimes birds show lines of white feathers around the eyes and over the head and these should be selected against as breeders as they are likely to cause white splashing in the plumage. Yellow or greenish bills must likewise be avoided since the first of these is a disqualification. In general this variety in breeding behaves insofar as color is concerned, very much like the Blue Andalusian chicken.[3] The young ducks when hatched are yellow or creamy blue and from blue matings there are also produced black and white ducklings. As in other colored breeds and varieties, the dark pin feathers are somewhat of a disadvantage from a market standpoint.

[Footnote 3: For a detailed discussion of the behaviour of the Blue Andalusian in breeding, the reader is referred to "The Mating and Breeding of Poultry" by Harry M. Lamon and Rob R. Slocum, published by the Orange Judd Publishing Company, New York City.]

The Crested White. Although not so large, this breed is much like the Pekin but with body carried more nearly horizontal and with a crest on the head. The type varies considerably however, the principal selection practiced having been for crest. The plumage is white in color throughout. What is desired in the crest is to have as large a one as possible, round and perfect in form, and set squarely on the head. Not infrequently crooked crests occur and also double or split crests, that is to say, where the crest is parted or divided. In some cases the crests may even come treble, that is, split into three parts. Entire absence of crest is by no means uncommon. In fact, it is considered a pretty good proportion if one half of the ducks hatched have crests although the matings vary considerably in this, occasionally one producing practically 100% of the offspring with crests. Avoid as breeders birds with small crests, lopped crests, split crests or showing an absence of crest. Avoid also breeders showing mottled or green bills in females and black bean in the bill of drakes.

The Buff. In type this breed is similar to the Swedish. As will be seen from the standard weights it is one of the medium sized breeds and makes a very nice market bird as it dresses out into a nice round fat carcass and is a good layer. In color the birds of both sexes should be as uniform a buff as possible except that the head and upper part of the neck in the drake should be seal brown when in full plumage. Color defects which are likely to be encountered and which should be avoided are the tendency for the head of the drake to run to a chestnut color and for his neck to be too light or faded out in color. Sometimes the head of the drake runs too dark in color approaching a greenish black like the head of the Rouen. This is of course undesirable. The wings of both sexes are apt to run to light or even in some cases, pure white flights. Blue wing bars are sometimes shown and these must be carefully avoided. Penciling such as is found in the Fawn and White Runner sometimes occurs and since it is a serious defect must be rigidly guarded against. Any tendency toward a white bib or a white ring around the neck of both sexes must likewise be avoided. Greenish or mottled bills must be avoided in ducks which are to be used as breeders. Not much trouble is experienced in the bill of drakes which as a rule comes good. Any blue cast in the feathers on the rump and back of both sexes must be selected against. As a rule the females of this breed tend to be better colored than the males. At certain periods of the moult the head coloring of the drakes becomes a good buff color and later when the moult is complete, it changes to a copper color. When hatched the ducklings are a creamy yellow.

The Runner. The type of this breed is quite different from that of the other breed of ducks and type is very important. The Runner wants to be decidedly upstanding and to be very reachy. It should have very slim slender lines. The neck should be straight and the head should be carried at right angles to the neck. The bill should be perfectly straight on top and on a line with the skull showing absolutely no tendency to be dished. The legs of this breed are longer than those of other ducks and this accounts for the fact that they run rather than waddle when they move about. It is from this fact that they get their name. They are very active and are troublesome about crawling through fences. They are good layers and non-sitters and they have often been called the Leghorns of the duck family. It must be remembered, however, that while they have the inherent ability to lay as well as hens they will do this only when they receive proper feed and care. It is quite useless to expect a high egg yield from them when they are carelessly fed and improperly housed and cared for. Avoid as breeders ducks of both sexes that are too heavy behind, or in other words, are too heavy-bottomed. Avoid birds which are too short in legs. Avoid crooked or sharp backs. Round heads must likewise be avoided.

The Fawn and White Runner. In this variety the markings must be very distinct and definite. There is a tendency which must be avoided for the head to run to black instead of chestnut, especially in males. It is likewise necessary to avoid females which tend to show penciling on the sides of the breast or on the wing-bows. These defects are apt to be associated with colored flight feathers which is also a defect to be avoided. Guard against too much fawn extending up the neck from the body to the head as the neck should be white in color. Too dark tail coverts approaching a greenish black sometimes occur and are undesirable. In type this variety will not average quite as good as the White.

The White Runner. This variety is best in type and it likewise runs good in color which should be white throughout. Sometimes foreign color will be shown in the back of females and this of course must be avoided. Also avoid birds as breeders with green or mottled bills.

The Penciled Runner. In type this variety runs about the same as the Fawn and White. The color combination is rather difficult to breed as it is hard to get the good penciling desired in the female together with the white markings. In general, in breeding this variety there is a tendency to pay more attention to type than to color. The penciling is like that of the Rouen but lighter in color consisting of a brown penciling on a fawn colored ground. Avoid any grayish stippling on the breast of the drake and also on the wing-bows. These defects are likely to be associated with colored flights which are undesirable. The colored portion of the head of the drake is darker than that of the duck in this variety. Avoid lack of white on the neck in both sexes and avoid females which are lacking in penciling.

Preparing Ducks for the Show. Aside from selecting the individuals which most nearly approach the standard requirements there is very little which can be done in the way of preparing the birds for the show as these fowls are practically self-prepared. For a period of at least a week or ten days before they are shipped to the show those intended for exhibition should be given access to a grass range and also if possible to running water. The grass range will keep them in good condition and the running water will allow them to clean themselves. Any broken feathers should be plucked at least six weeks before the birds are to be shown in order to allow the feathers time enough to grow out again. It must be remembered that most ducks after getting in a good condition of flesh do not tend to hold this for a very long period but soon grow thinner again and will not take on fat the second time for some little period.

Often there will be a difference in weight as high as 3 pounds when a duck is in good condition and after it has thinned. In order to have the ducks in top form, therefore, it is necessary to bring them up to flesh at the proper time. In order to bring ducks which are to be exhibited up to standard weight, they should be fed twice daily, for at least 10 days before shipping, a grain mixture consisting of one part corn and two parts oats. Give them all they will eat of this mixture. With Runners and the small breeds of ducks there is a danger of their putting on too much weight if corn is used in the ration and it is therefore best to give them oats alone. When the birds are shipped to the show they are quite likely to get their plumage soiled during the journey. When this occurs fill a barrel about half full of water. Then as the ducks are taken out of the shipping coops take three of them at a time, put them in the barrel and cover it over, leaving them for a few minutes. When they are taken out they will usually be clean.

Catching and Handling Ducks

Ducks should never be caught by the legs which are short and weak and are very likely to be injured. For the same reason they should never be carried by the legs. Ducks should be caught by the neck, grasping them just below the head. They can be carried short distances without injury in this way but it is not advisable to carry fat ducks by the neck for any considerable distance. The best way to handle them is to catch them by the neck, then carry them on the arm with the legs in the hand just as one would carry a chicken. See Fig. 15. A scoop net about 18 inches in diameter and with a six foot handle can also be used to excellent advantage in catching ducks.

Packing and Shipping Hatching Eggs

Eggs for hatching must be shipped when they are fresh as duck eggs tend to deteriorate in quality quite rapidly. They may be shipped fairly long distances. Shipment may be made either by express or by Parcel Post. In order to prevent breakage and to lessen the effects of the jar to which the eggs are subjected during shipment, they must be carefully packed. One of the best methods is to use an ordinary market basket. Line the basket well on the bottom and sides with excelsior. Wrap each egg in paper and then wrap in excelsior so that there will be a good thick cushion of excelsior between the eggs and they will not be allowed to come in contact with one another. Pack the eggs in the basket securely standing them on end so that they cannot move or shift around. Cover the top of the eggs with a thick layer of excelsior using enough so that it runs up well above the sides of the basket. Over the top sew a piece of strong cotton cloth. Instead of sewing the cloth it can be pushed up under the outside rim of the basket with a case knife, this being quicker and equally as effective as sewing.

CHAPTER III

Commercial Duck Farming--Location--Estimate of Equipment and Capital Necessary in Starting the Business

Distribution. Commercial Duck farming is confined very largely to the sections within easy shipping distance of the larger cities. A great majority of these farms are located about New York City, particularly on Long Island. Some duck farms are located on the Pacific Coast and a few commercial plants are scattered about here and there throughout the country. The size of these farms ranges all the way from plants with an output of 5,000 or 10,000 ducklings up to those with an output around 100,000 yearly.

Stock Used. The stock used on the commercial duck plants of the United States consists exclusively of the Pekin. The reasons for the use of this particular breed are the fact that it has white plumage and therefore dresses out well, that it is of good size, that its egg production is good, and that it makes quick growth.

Location of Plant. On Long Island the commercial duck plants are located along the streams, especially those on the southern shore of the Island, which empty into the various bays. Locations along these streams are not easy to secure at the present time owing to the fact that duck farms are not allowed in many sections where summer homes have been built. A water site of this sort is very valuable, although not absolutely essential, since it provides water yards for the breeding ducks and for the fattening ducklings if desired, and reduces the labor and cost of equipment materially since the ducks always have access to water and no additional provision need be made to provide them with drinking water. It also enables the ducks to keep their plumage clean. Usually these locations are on fresh water streams but some of them are further out toward the bay where the water is salty or at least brackish.

The mature ducks thrive well on the salt water and do not have to be furnished with fresh drinking water in addition. For the young ducks, however, with a salt water location it is necessary to provide fresh drinking water. A few farms in other sections of the country are what are known as dry land farms, that is to say, they are not situated on the bank of a stream. In such locations running water is carried through the yards so that the ducks have an ample supply of drinking water and in some cases artificial ponds are constructed to provide water in which the breeding ducks can swim. Formerly the idea was universally held that swimming water was essential for the breeders in order to secure good fertility, and many duck farmers still believe that better results can be secured in this way. On some of the dry land duck farms, however, breeding ducks are successfully kept without such swimming places. The young market ducklings do not require water to swim in although some raisers prefer to have it and it is commonly allowed where readily available. On the dry land farms provision is made simply for a continuous supply of fresh drinking water for the fattening ducklings. Ducklings kept out of the water, do not take as much exercise and, in consequence, fatten a little more readily.

Making a Start in Duck Farming

Duck farms or plants are sometimes operated on a considerable scale at the beginning, the plans being carefully laid by some experienced duck man. In these cases, operations at the start may be of sufficient magnitude so that the output will amount to 15,000 or 20,000 ducklings in a year. In most cases, however, these places have been the result of a more gradual growth from a small beginning, a condition made necessary either by the inexperience of the grower or by lack of capital. Not infrequently men engaged in other forms of farming but possessing a suitable location will keep 200 or 300 breeding ducks and from this gradually build up a good sized duck plant.

Equipment, Capital, etc. Required. The estimates given as to the amount of equipment and capital required are based on the assumption that a plant is to be operated of sufficient size to have a yearly output of about 30,000 ducklings. It must be understood in this connection that location and various other conditions or circumstances will influence the cost of different items of equipment and for this reason these estimates must not be considered as absolute but should rather serve as a guide or basis on which to figure. The figures here given contemplate the building up of an establishment which is efficient but which is in no particular elaborate, the buildings and other equipment being as simple and inexpensive as possible.

Lay-out or Arrangement of the Plant. The plant must be carefully planned so as to make the best possible use of the land and particularly of the water frontage. It is particularly important to arrange the buildings in such a manner as to cut down labor as much as possible. If there is any expectation of enlarging the capacity at some future time, this must also be borne in mind in the arrangement of the various buildings and yards. The incubator cellar should be convenient to the No. 1 brooder house and the various brooder houses to one another. The brooder house must likewise be convenient to the growing and fattening houses and yards and these in turn to the killing house. The feed room should be centrally located so as to save labor as much as possible in feeding the ducks.

Land Required. For a duck plant of the size indicated 10 acres of land should be ample. This, however, means that no effort would be made to grow any of the feed for the ducks or ducklings with the exception of green feed. In some cases where the lay of the land is unusually favorable so that the plant can be laid out to the very best advantage, a smaller amount of ground than this might be sufficient but it is not well to figure on less than 10 acres.

Number of Breeders Required. With the usual methods of management and with good success, one may estimate that 40 young ducks can be marketed each year from each breeding female. This is a good average although in some good years duck raisers will do a little better than this. On the other hand in poor years they will not do so well. For a plant having an output of 30,000 market ducks there would therefore be needed in the neighborhood of 800 breeding ducks in addition to 100 drakes.

Housing Required for Breeders. In figuring on the amount of housing required for this number of breeding ducks, it is necessary to figure on 2?to 3 square feet of floor space per bird, 3 square feet being better than 2? This would require a housing space 20 feet deep by 120 feet long. However ducks are not usually housed in one building of this size, and in fact it is better not to do so since the smaller the flock of breeders kept together the better they will do. In no case should a duck raiser run more than 400 ducks in a flock and it is very much better to run them in pens of 100 each. In fact, some breeders do not place more than 25 to 50 breeding ducks in a pen.

Incubator Capacity. Incubators are used exclusively for hatching the eggs. At the present time in practically all cases some form of hot water mammoth incubator is utilized for this purpose. An investment is required both in incubators and in a cellar in which to operate them. In figuring on the incubator capacity necessary to take care of a proposition of this size, it is necessary to base the estimate on the number of eggs produced during the season of flush production. The duck raiser figures on incubating all eggs suitable for the purpose rather than to sell any of them for other purposes as there is a greater profit in rearing and marketing the ducklings. For that reason he must have incubator capacity enough to take care of all the eggs laid at any time of the year. During the season of flush production the yield will ordinarily run in the neighborhood of 80%. The period of incubation is 28 days but 2 days more should be added to this to allow for cleaning out the machines, etc., before starting another hatch. This means that there would be 30 days between hatches. Figuring on 800 ducks with an 80% production for 30 days an incubator capacity of around 19,200 eggs would be required.

Brooder Capacity. A brooder house capacity, where artificial heat can be supplied, sufficient to take care of about half of the total output of the plant at one time is necessary. This means there would have to be on this plant a heated brooder house capacity for 15,000 ducklings. About half of this number or 7500 would need accommodations in the number 1 or warmest brooder house where the heat can be kept up to 65 or 70 degrees in the house itself, and warmer of course under the hover. The other 7500 ducklings capacity would be in the number 2 house, that is, a house where heat could be supplied in the early spring and where the temperature could be run up to 60 degrees. Hovers in such a house are not really needed but it is common to cover the hot waterpipes with a platform in order to provide a runway on which one can run a wheel barrow and thus simplify feeding. Ordinarily after May 1 no heat is needed in the number 2 brooder house. The young ducks are usually 2 to 3 weeks old when they go into the number 2 house and they stay there for about 2 weeks depending on the weather. Heat for the brooder houses is supplied by means of hot water pipes and a coal burning stove such as are used in brooder houses for chickens. A number 3 or cold brooder house is also needed where ducklings can be housed and can be driven in at night and in cold weather after they have graduated from the number 2 house. From the number 3 house a part of the ducklings are taken directly to the yards where they are housed in open front sheds.

Fattening Houses or Sheds. In addition to the brooder houses, there are required fattening houses or sheds for the ducks when they are moved from the No. 3 brooder house to the yards. Suitable houses for this purpose are 16 feet deep by 24 feet long. In front they are 5 feet high and in the rear 3?feet. They are set on posts with a base board around to make them tight. The fronts are entirely open and provided with curtains which are used only in the winter to keep out the snow. The ducklings are shut in these houses when desired by means of wire panels which close the lower part of the front. Houses such as described are divided into two parts and each side will accommodate 200 ducklings.

Feed Storage. Considerable feed storage room is necessary as it is very desirable to be able to buy feed in quantity and also to carry a considerable stock on hand in order to offset the possibility of not being able to secure feed at any time. There should be storage capacity for 4 cars of 30 tons each, in other words, for 120 tons of feed. Still greater capacity than this is desirable. In connection with the feed storage there should be a place where the feed can be mixed and where feed can be cooked. Two power operated feed mixers are required as one is not sufficient during the busy season to allow the mixing and feeding of the mash for both the breeders and the young stock at the same time. A feed cutter is necessary in preparing the green feed which is mixed in the mash. The usual type of kettle feed cooker is commonly used for boiling fish and preparing other cooked feeds but in its place a small four-horse steam boiler can be utilized to good advantage as this makes it possible to cook the feed right in the mixer by using a steam hose.

Killing and Picking House. A killing and picking house where the ducks can be prepared for market is another necessary building but this need not be an expensive building. It must be located with reference to its convenience to the rest of the plant. It is also desirable to locate it over a spring if one is available for the spring water can be used to excellent advantage in cooling the dressed ducklings. When a spring is not available water must be piped to this building. The killing house is usually built with at least one side open or partly open. A place is provided outside the picking room where the ducks can be hung and bled. Inside room is required for six or eight pickers. A kettle for heating water to be used in scalding the ducks is necessary as are also tanks in which to place the ducks after they are picked. Additional room is needed where the ducks can be weighed and packed ready for shipment.

Residence. In addition to the other buildings enumerated, a residence would of course be necessary. The size and elaborateness of this and consequently its cost depends entirely upon the owner's needs and wishes.

Horse Power. One horse and wagon for the purpose of drawing the feed about the plant and for certain other necessary work would be required. If the owner desires to do his own hauling of the feed from the railroad and the other necessary trucking he would, of course, have to keep more horses, a team at least, or an automobile truck. Where only one horse is kept, this trucking must be hired done.

Feeding Track. On many of the larger duck farms, a feed track is employed in feeding the stock. Such a track consists of a framework of sufficient strength to support a car filled with mash which is pushed along the track by hand. The track leads from the feed mixer across the various yards where the ducks to be fed are located, including both the breeding ducks, yard ducks and brooder ducks in yards. This involves a considerable amount of trackage which must be fairly level and which runs over the yard fences or along the ends of the yards so that the feed can be shoveled directly from the car into the feeding trays in the yards. The use of a feed track simplifies the feeding considerably but its construction is quite expensive. Where a track is not used, the feed as mixed is dumped into a low wagon which is driven along the yards, or through them by removing movable panels in the fences and the feed shoveled from the wagon to the feed trays.

Electric Lights. Most duck farms at the present time are located where electric lighting is available. It is desirable and in fact almost necessary to have the various houses wired so that lights can be turned on when desired. In addition, lights are usually provided in the yards for fattening ducks and are used at night and especially during storms to keep the ducks from stampeding.

Water Supply. An adequate water supply is essential. This will consist of a well or spring furnishing an ample amount of water, a power pump and a water supply tank. From the tank, the water must be piped to the incubator cellar, the brooder houses, the killing house, the feed house and to any of the yards where the ducks do not have access to a natural supply of good water. In addition, of course, the water from the same tank is usually used to supply the residence.

Fences. Not a great deal of investment is necessary in fences since the yards are rather small and the fences are low. Two-foot fences of two-inch mesh wire are used for the yard ducks while for the little ducks 18-inch wire of one-inch mesh is used. The biggest items of expense connected with the fences are the cost of the stakes or posts used in their construction and the labor used in this work. The portion of the yards extending into the water are the most troublesome and most expensive to build. In some cases, rather elaborate wooden picket fences are used in the water yards. These are more permanent but are more expensive to build.

Labor. For a plant of the size indicated there would be required in addition to an active working proprietor three other men. One man would be needed to operate the incubators, one man would devote his time to the brooder houses, one man would feed the yard ducks and the fattening pens, and one man would do the killing and packing, take care of the feathers, clean the yards, etc. Of course, there would be periods when these men would not have their entire time taken up with their particular duties and this would permit them to turn in and help with the miscellaneous work on the plant.

In addition to the regular men employed, additional labor would be necessary to do the picking. For this purpose pickers are usually brought in and work by the piece. During the spring of 1920 these pickers received six cents per duck and they will average about 75 ducks a day, beginning work at 6 in the morning and finishing by noon or a little later. Some pickers will average as high as 100 ducks a day. In the busy season from 800 to 1200 ducks will be marketed per week and the usual practice is to kill and pick not over three days a week, usually during the first part of the week.

Invested Capital. Investment in the business exclusive of working capital, that is to say, the money in the land and buildings and other equipment would require under present conditions about $1,000 for each thousand ducks marketed. In other words, in a plant of this size, close to $30,000 would be invested. The amount of invested capital depends to some extent upon location and upon the elaborateness of the buildings and other equipment but with a well laid out economical plant an investment of the size indicated should be sufficient.

Working Capital. In addition to the capital invested in the plant there would be required a considerable amount of working capital. From the first of November to the beginning of the marketing of the ducks there would be required from $6,000 to $8,000 with which to purchase feed, meet the pay roll, and for other running expenses. Even after the marketing begins there would be a period of from a month to six weeks when the expenses will continue to be greater than the receipts so that some additional capital might be necessary. However, returns would begin to come in which could be used to take care of the more pressing current obligations so that additional working capital which might be needed over that indicated would not be large.

Profits. The profits in commercial duck raising vary widely, as must be expected, depending upon the management, upon the season and upon prices received. After deducting all overhead charges and interest on the investment, the net return per duck should be at least 10 cents per duckling marketed. In fact the return should be 15 cents to provide much inducement to engage in the business. Some seasons the returns will run greater than this but on the other hand, there is always the chance of occasional big losses.

CHAPTER IV

Commercial Duck Farming--Management of the Breeding Stock

Age of Breeders. On most large commercial duck plants the entire breeding stock is renewed each year. In other words, the breeders are kept only through their first laying season. This makes it necessary to select from the young stock reared and save for breeders as many head as it is desired to carry for the coming year. This practice is used for the reason that ducks lay best during their first year. Therefore, since it is desired to keep up the maximum egg production in order to raise as many market ducks as possible, young breeders are considered better. Some raisers, however, keep a part of their breeding ducks for two years and occasionally for 3 or even 4 years but this is not the usual practice. Recent comparison made between young and two year old ducks as breeders would seem to indicate that ducklings hatched from the eggs of the latter live a little better.

Distinguishing Young from Old Ducks. In this connection it is of interest to know how young ducks can be readily distinguished from the older birds. The young ducks have bright yellow legs and bills while the old ducks after a period of laying, lose a considerable amount of the yellow from these sections. In addition, soon after the ducks begin to lay, their bills as a rule will begin to be streaked with black. Young ducks can also be told from the old ducks by feeling of the end of the breast bone which runs to a point at the abdomen. In the older ducks this is hard while in the young ducks it is gristly and bends easily. The windpipe of an old duck is hard and rather difficult to compress or dent while in the young duck it is softer and easily dented.

Selection of Breeding Ducks. The breeders are usually selected from the ducklings which reach market age from the last week in June through July. As these lots become ready for market and are driven into the pens to be slaughtered each duck is handled and any especially good birds which the proprietor thinks will make good breeders are thrown out at this time.

In making selection of breeders those are chosen which are healthy and thrifty and which have good wide, long and deep bodies. Ducks with crooked wings, crooked tails, hump backs or paddle legs are rejected for this purpose. After the young ducks for breeders are selected they are put in a yard or fattening pen until the number which the owner expects to keep is complete. These young breeders generally begin to moult soon after they are selected and from this time on they are fed whole corn and plenty of green feed until it is time to begin feeding the laying ration. Some of the breeding ducks will usually begin to lay about December 1 although they will not lay heavily at that time. The laying ration described later should be begun about that time or a couple of weeks earlier.

Number of Females to a Drake. As a rule on commercial duck farms the birds are mated in the proportion of about one drake to seven ducks. This proportion will vary to some extent under different methods of management and weather conditions and may run all the way from 1 to 5 to 1 to 8. The smaller number of drakes should be used late in the season while the larger number will give better fertility early in the breeding season.

Since the drakes do not fight seriously, flock matings can be made. Better results will be obtained from smaller flocks than from large flocks and there will also be less cracked eggs and less very dirty eggs from the smaller flocks. Before the ducks are let out in the morning there is a tendency for them to run back and forth through the pens, and in this way they tramp over many of the eggs which are laid anywhere about the floor. The larger the flock the more cracked and dirty eggs will result. While the drakes do not fight each other they do at times injure and kill the ducks to some extent when three or four drakes may chase one duck. In this way they may injure the ducks' backs and often pick their eyes and necks. Whenever a duck is found which is injured she should be removed from the flock. Difficulty of this sort is most prevalent about the 1st of March. If the trouble gets very bad it can be stopped to some extent by cutting back the upper bills of the drakes about one-fourth of an inch with a tinsnip or by reducing the proportion of drakes.

Securing Breeding Drakes. It is common practice on duck plants to avoid inbreeding by securing drakes from some other flock each year. This is usually accomplished by buying the drakes outright from some neighboring duck farmer. It may also be accomplished by purchasing a few eggs for hatching in order to secure new blood. In any particular community there is a tendency for the duck farmers to trade breeding drakes among themselves for a period of years with the result that they all have much the same blood and not a great deal of benefit is obtained from securing the drakes from some neighbor's flock. It is undoubtedly good practice to go farther afield occasionally for a supply of breeding drakes. In purchasing stock for new blood be sure that it is as good as the home stock and better if it can be found. It will do no good to purchase and use inferior stock and may do much harm.

Houses and Yards for Breeders

The breeding flocks are usually confined to breeding yards. The size of these yards depends upon the size of the breeding flock but large yards are not required. A yard for 200 breeders is not as a rule larger than 100 by 200 feet including the water part of the yard. Houses and yards should be located on sand if possible as this is easier to keep clean and therefore keeps the birds in better condition. Occasional flocks of breeding ducks are allowed their liberty but this is not common practice nor is it good practice unless the surroundings are clean and the ducks do not have access to stagnant mud or refuse in which they can work. If ducks work too much in this kind of material they will eat more or less of it which injures the eggs for hatching purposes.

Many different styles of houses are used for breeders, some of which are decidedly more elaborate than is necessary. A very satisfactory economical house is one 20 feet deep, 7 feet high in front and 4 feet at back, with a shed roof. This can be constructed of tongue and groove material or may be made of unmatched stuff and covered with paper. A house of this proportion makes a good light house and it can be carried in length according to the size of the flock. For a breeding unit of 200 ducks, which is a good unit to use, a house 20 feet deep and 30 to 40 feet long is suitable. No floor is used in the house but it should be well filled up with dirt so that the water will not come in.

One or more good sized openings are left in the front of the breeding house for ventilation, or windows may be placed in the front which can be used for this purpose. Good ventilation is necessary. Additional ventilation is secured from the doors. If the weather is mild the doors are left partly open, if cold they are nearly closed, while when the weather is hot they are left entirely open. A good scheme is to use a sort of Dutch door so that the bottom or top half can be opened independently. In this way the top part of the doors can be left open so as to let in the sunlight and still keep the ducks in the house or the top may be left closed and the bottom opened so as to allow the ducks to go in or out and still cut down the amount of ventilation. When the weather is warm the doors may be left entirely open except for a board 18 inches to 2 feet wide inserted in the bottom of the door when it is desired to keep the ducks in.

Shade is essential for the breeders and if not provided naturally by trees must be supplied by means of artificial shelters.

Bedding and Cleaning the Breeding Houses. Usually straw, meadow hay, or swale hay is used for bedding. Shavings make good material for this purpose if they do not contain too much sawdust. The principal objection to shavings is that it takes longer to bed with them. Often a few joists are laid at the back of the house on which to pile bales of straw or other bedding so that it will be kept dry and will serve as an emergency supply available for bedding the house in stormy days. The houses should be bedded fairly often in order to keep the floors clean and dry and so as not to allow the ducks' feet to get cold. The frequency with which bedding is necessary will depend upon the weather. In winter it may at times be necessary to bed every day. In May it may be necessary only twice a week and still later in the season only once a week. In wet weather the ducks track in lots of mud and water and frequent bedding helps to keep the eggs clean. The houses are cleaned out only once a year and this is usually done after the ducks have stopped laying. To clean out the houses while the ducks are laying would disturb them and tend to stop their egg production.

Cleaning the Breeding Yards. The yards should be cleaned whenever they need it, that is, whenever they begin to get sloppy or sticky. It is a matter of judgment to decide when this is necessary. The character of the soil influences this, as sandy yards absorb the droppings better and do not need cleaning as frequently as heavier soils. In the yards for the breeding ducks, or the water yards, this will as a rule not be over 2 or 3 times a season. In dry weather cleaning is accomplished by sweeping the yards with a broom. In wet weather the droppings spread over the yard and are packed down by the ducks' feet until they form a layer of putty-like material which cannot be swept off but is scraped off by means of a hoe.

Water Yards for Breeders. Formerly it was the consensus of opinion that breeders needed water in which they could swim in order to keep in good breeding condition and to give the best results in fertility of the eggs. At present it is not considered necessary to have sufficient water to permit swimming although many breeders prefer to do this and feel that they get better results from it. However, breeding ducks have been and are being kept successfully in dry yards where water is supplied to them simply in an amount sufficient to allow them to drink and to clean themselves. Where water yards are provided this should not be on stagnant water but there should be some circulation of the water so as to keep it clean and fresh. Where the lay of the land is such that it is not possible to run all the yards down to a stream for this purpose it is sometimes possible to dig a canal or ditch from the stream to the yards so as to allow the ducks access to the water. Where the yards can extend into the water it saves a great deal of labor or considerable expense in equipment as it is not then necessary to provide the ducks with drinking water by means of some artificial arrangement such as a concrete gutter or ditch extending through the yards or by means of artificial ponds.

If the water yards used freeze over in winter it is necessary to cut holes in the ice so that the ducks can get water for drinking purposes. Sometimes the ducks will go into these water holes and after getting their plumage wet will come out and sit down in the yard and freeze fast to the ground. During such weather conditions it is necessary to make the rounds of the yards frequently and to loosen any ducks that have frozen fast. If they are left in that condition they are apt to injure themselves in trying to pull free and if left too long will die.

Feeding the Breeders. Breeding ducks are fed twice a day, in the morning and at night. It is usual practice to feed the breeders last in the morning and first at night. The reason for feeding them last in the morning is that they are usually fed in the yards rather than the house and they should be kept in until they are through laying which will be after daylight. A good breeding ration consists of the following, the proportions being given by measure in bushels.

1 bushel bran. 1 bushel low-grade flour. 1 bushel corn meal. 1 bushel green feed. ?bushel either raw or cooked vegetables. 1 bushel in 10 of beef scrap. ?bushel in 10 of cooked fish.

This ration will keep the breeding ducks in good flesh but there will be no difficulty in their getting too fat. It is also a good laying ration and will promote good egg production. The vegetables used in this ration usually consist of sugar beets, cow beets, potatoes, etc. However, if potatoes are used the amount of flour in the ration should be reduced a little so as not to make the ration too heavy. Beets, when used, are fed raw cut up and mixed in the feed. Small potatoes, boiled and mixed in the feed are more valuable as they have a greater food value than beets. Some duck growers feed fish entirely, using no beef scrap. This is done where a plentiful supply of fish can be secured by going out into the bay after them. However, this is not very good practice for a sufficient supply of fish may not always be available and the ducks are so fond of the fish that they will not eat well the beef scrap used as a substitute for the fish, until they have become used to it. Fish is prepared for feeding by boiling it thoroughly in a feed cooker.

The available land on the plant is used to grow a supply of green feed. Rye is used for this purpose early in the spring as soon as it is high enough to mow. It is mowed the first time when it is like a lawn. At this stage it does not have to be cut up. Oats are used in the same way. During the summer fodder corn is used. This is the poorest crop for the purpose but is as a rule the only one available at that time. Rape is sowed in August and its use begun about the time of the first frost and kept up until the hard freezes come or until it is buried under the snow. Creek grass which is secured from the fresh water streams on Long Island by going out in a flat bottom boat and raking it off the creek bottom with a wooden rake, is very much relished by the ducks and is used whenever it is available. However, the supply of this material is not as plentiful as it was formerly and it is rather hard to get. When it is available it can be used either in winter or summer.

Good field clover cut up and boiled with the potatoes or with the fish makes a good green feed. All of these green materials for use in the ration, unless they are already in short lengths, are cut up by means of a power feed cutter before they are mixed in the mash. When no other form of green feed is available ground alfalfa is used but only half as much of this material is mixed with the ration as is used of any of the other kinds of green feed. Wherever possible the various duck yards should be used to grow a crop of green stuff such as oats or rye as this not only helps out on the supply of green feed but also helps to sweeten the soil. The growing of a crop on the heavier types of soil used for ducks is especially important as such soils are more likely to become contaminated from the droppings.

The ration for the ducks is mixed up in a power feed mixer which works much on the principle of a power dough mixer. In fact, dough mixers are used on some plants. In mixing the feed enough water should be added to bring the material to a consistency where it will hold together when squeezed in the hand. In fact, the consistency should be between crumbly and sticky, but should never be sloppy. The feed is dumped from the mixer into a low horse drawn wagon and driven around to the various yards where it is shoveled off on to the feed troughs or trays. On some large duck plants a track is provided which runs over the yards and over this a car loaded with feed is pushed and the feed shoveled into the feed trays.

The breeders should be fed in the same place. If feeding is begun in the house this practice should be continued. If feeding is begun in the yards it should be continued there. To change disturbs the ducks and interferes with their egg production.

Coarse ground oyster shell about as large as corn should be kept before the breeders all the time in boxes where they can help themselves. A flock of 700 or 800 breeders will eat upwards of 200 pounds a week of this material. Unless sand is available in the yards where they can get it, ducks should also have access to a supply of good sharp creek sand but when kept in sand yards no other form of grit need be furnished.

The usual method of feeding is to utilize flat troughs on which the feed is shoveled. Only as much feed should be given at the regular feeding time as the ducks will eat up clean. This makes it necessary to watch the feeding carefully and to regulate the amount accordingly. It is good practice to gather up any feed that is left by the ducks so that it will not lie there to sour and spoil as such feed is bad for the birds.

Egg Production

The average egg production of Pekin ducks kept under commercial farm conditions will run from 80 to 125 eggs per head for the season. This will vary somewhat from year to year and also with the management and feed given the ducks. The laying begins to a small extent about December 1 and gradually increases until the ducks are laying freely in February. As the hot weather of summer begins to come on the laying drops off until about July 1 and after this not enough eggs are produced as a rule to pay to hold the breeding ducks longer. Often many ducks will stop laying considerably before this, especially those which have started laying early and it may not pay to keep such pens later than May. Laying takes place early in the morning and practically all the eggs are laid soon after daylight. It is for this reason that the ducks are usually shut up at night so that all the eggs laid will be secured as some of them would otherwise be lost by their being laid around in the yard or in the water. In the spring the ducks can be let out about 6 a. m., as the laying will be pretty well over by that time, but in winter they must be kept shut up later in order to secure all the eggs. After the ducks start laying in the spring they are very regular and continuous layers and will miss fewer days than most hens.

After the breeding ducks are first put in the breeding pens and shut in the houses at night it is common practice to use electric lights for the first 2 or 3 weeks in order to keep them from stampeding as ducks in strange surroundings are quite nervous and are quite likely to stampede and to run over one another thus causing cripples. Electric lights have also been used to some extent during the late fall and winter for the purpose of inducing egg production earlier than the natural season. As a rule the ducks can be started to laying about 4 weeks after turning on the lights but the average production under this system is not likely to run more than 60 eggs for the season as so handled they moult quite early in the spring. A single 25 watt light is sufficient for a house or pen 16 ?24 feet and the lights are left turned on all night.

The object in feeding and caring for the breeding ducks is to keep them from moulting and to keep them laying as long as possible. It must be remembered that any radical change in feed or manner of feeding, shutting them up too closely, change of temperature, or other disturbing conditions are likely to cause moulting and to check egg production. Any change in feed must be made carefully and gradually, not suddenly. It must also be remembered that ducks are excitable birds and must be handled and driven carefully so as to disturb them as little as possible.

Time of Marketing Breeders

The breeders should be turned off to market whenever their egg production drops off so decidedly that it no longer pays to hold them. In most cases this will be about the 1st of July but it may range considerably earlier than this, especially with pens of ducks that have started laying early. When the ducks finish laying their eggs they begin to moult and it is at this time that they should be marketed. If marketing is delayed, the ducks will lose condition as the moulting progresses and will therefore be held at a loss.

Diseases and Pests

Disease. Old ducks, that is, mature ducks, are practically free from disease. Of course, there will be a certain amount of loss in the breeding stock from various causes but this should not run for the entire season more than 10% of the flock. Ducks do not become egg bound, but sometimes, especially during heavy laying, they become ruptured.

Insect Pests. Ducks are remarkably free from lice and other insect pests and those which they do have do not trouble them much. It is unnecessary therefore to take any precautions in the way of treating the ducks to keep them free of insects.

Dogs. Occasionally trouble may be experienced from dogs. If these animals get into the yards with the breeders or the fattening ducks, they may kill a good many and in addition will seriously injure the rest by chasing them and by the fright which the ducks are given.

CHAPTER V

Commercial Duck Farming--Incubation

The Pekin duck is essentially a non-broody breed. It, therefore, becomes necessary to resort to incubators for the purpose of hatching the eggs. Occasional ducks will sit if allowed to do so but it is not the practice on commercial duck farms to allow them to sit and hatch their young. No special means are taken to break them of broodiness other than not to allow them eggs to sit on.

Kinds of Incubators Used. Both the smaller kerosene lamp heated incubators and the large or mammoth hot water heated incubators are used for hatching duck eggs. At the present time the mammoth hot water machines are those which are in principal use due largely to the lessened labor required to operate them.

Incubator Cellar. It is necessary to provide some room in which the incubators can be installed and operated. This may take the form of a cellar, or the incubators may be operated in rooms above the ground. Many of the incubator cellars on duck farms are only partially under ground and not a few of them are built entirely out of ground. The particular size and shape of the cellar or incubator room will, of course, depend upon the number of incubators to be installed and upon their make and shape. Usually these buildings are constructed with rather thick walls so that the temperature of the room will fluctuate less with changes in outside temperature. Provision is also necessary by means of windows or other ventilating devices to provide for good ventilation in the room. The cellars are usually constructed with cement floors as moisture is used freely and wooden floors would rot out quickly.

Incubator Capacity Required. The aim on commercial duck farms is to hatch all of the eggs produced which are suitable for the purpose. Practically no eggs are sold except the cracked eggs or those which would not give good results in the incubator such as too large or too small eggs. Occasionally, of course, there will be sales of duck eggs in comparatively large lots for incubation purposes where someone is starting a duck farm. Occasionally also duck farmers buy from each other a few eggs for incubation in order to secure new blood. On the whole, however, practically all of the eggs laid are incubated and it is necessary to have an incubator capacity sufficient to take care of the eggs as they are produced during the flush season.

Since the egg production at this time will run around about 80% and since the period of incubation is 28 days and a couple more days must be allowed to take the ducklings out of the machines and to clean up the machines, it is necessary to figure on 30 days between hatches. To take care of the flush production at this time there would be required an incubator capacity of from 20 to 25 eggs per head of breeding ducks. The latter figure is a safer estimate than the former. Of course, eggs sufficient to fill the entire incubator capacity are not put in the machines at any one time but different lots are put in as soon as a sufficient number is obtained to make it worth while. There will be, therefore, eggs in various stages of incubation in different sections of the machines at the same time. While Pekin duck eggs will run about ?heavier in weight than hens' eggs they do not take up a proportionately greater amount of space in the incubator. An incubator tray will accommodate about 5/6 as many Pekin duck eggs as it will hens' eggs.

Age of Hatching Eggs. Duck eggs should be set as often as enough are secured to fill one or more trays in the incubator or enough to produce a sufficient number of ducklings to utilize brooding space to advantage. Since duck eggs deteriorate more rapidly than hens' eggs they cannot be kept so long before they are set. It is best not to save them for longer than one week. During the season of flush production it is not, of course, necessary to save them that long since enough eggs will be secured to set each day if desired. The usual practice at this time is to set twice a week. During the early part of the season when the production of eggs is low and the temperature cool the eggs are often saved for as long a period as two weeks without noticeably bad results.

Care of Hatching Eggs. Eggs for hatching should be kept in a cool place. Any place suitable for keeping hens' eggs for hatching is a suitable place for duck eggs. The temperature should be from 50?to 70?Fahrenheit. Where the eggs are not kept longer than one week, it is not necessary to turn them, especially if they are kept on end. If kept longer than this it is safer to turn them once a day or once in two days, handling them carefully so as not to crack any or to injure their hatching qualities.

Selecting the Eggs for Hatching. Medium sized eggs are preferred for this purpose. Therefore, the extremely large eggs and the very small ones are thrown out. Rough shelled eggs or eggs with crooked or deformed shells are likewise thrown out since they are not likely to hatch well. Eggs that are badly soiled so that they cannot be tested easily are washed but the clean eggs are not. All the eggs intended for incubation purposes are sounded by striking them gently against one another in order to detect and remove the cracked eggs. No selection is made on the basis of color. The eggs may be white, creamy white or a blue, or bluish green in color. At the present time a considerably less proportion of the eggs show a blue tint than formerly. As the egg laying season advances the eggs laid by the ducks tend to get a little larger.

Temperature. Up to the time of testing, that is, about the fifth day, the incubator is run at a temperature of from 101 to 102 degrees. After the fifth day the temperature is kept as near 103 as possible. The most sensitive period for a duck egg is during the first 3 or 4 days of incubation. If they are allowed to get too warm during this time the germ may be killed while if the temperature is too low, development will be retarded.

Position of the Thermometer. In figuring on the proper temperature at which to run the incubator, the thermometer should be so placed that the bulb is on a level with the top of the eggs, preferably touching a fertile egg. If the thermometer bulb rests on an infertile egg the temperature recorded will be lower than the actual temperature of fertile eggs in the later stages of incubation, due to the animal heat of the developing embryos, with the result that the machine would be operated at too high a temperature.

Testing. It is common practice to make only one complete test. This is done on the evening of the fifth day. Testing may be done by means of an ordinary candling device such as is used with hens' eggs, each egg being examined separately. To save time a piece of apparatus may be used which is simple in construction and which simplifies the process of candling considerably. This may be termed a testing table. It consists of a table the same width as an incubator tray and longer than the tray. In the table there is an opening the size of a row of eggs and beneath this are placed several electric light bulbs with reflectors back of them so as to throw the light up through the eggs. By sliding the tray along the table each row of eggs is brought over the lights and their condition can be quickly noted. At this test all the infertile eggs are taken out as well as any eggs in which the germs have died. The infertile eggs after a careful retest are then packed in cases and sent to market where they are usually sold to bakers as tested eggs. While no second test is made of the eggs left in the machines the experienced incubator operator is constantly on the watch for and is constantly removing any eggs which die at a later time. To the experienced eye the color of the egg indicates that it has died as it takes on a sort of pinkish or darkish tint. Duck eggs after they die will spoil very quickly and must be removed promptly as the odor which they throw off is very strong and will prove harmful to the other eggs. The inexperienced operator can readily locate dead eggs by smelling over the tray.

Turning the Eggs. The eggs are neither turned, cooled nor otherwise disturbed after they are put in the incubator until after they are tested on the fifth day. From this time on they are turned twice a day, morning and night, until they begin to pip.

Cooling the Eggs. There is a considerable difference in the practice of incubator operators with regard to cooling. No cooling should be done until after the first test. After this some incubator men cool the eggs by dropping the doors of the machine. Others take the trays of eggs out and put them on top of the machine. Cooling is usually done once a day. The amount of cooling which the eggs require seems to vary greatly and here again the judgment of the operator comes into play. About the best general rule which can be given is that the eggs should be cooled until they do not feel warm to the face but they should never be cooled to the extent that they feel cold to the face or hands. The length of time to bring this about varies with the age of the eggs and the temperature of the room.

Moisture. A good deal of moisture is used in incubating duck eggs. It is usual to begin to spray the eggs with water the next day after testing. However, this may vary anywhere from the sixth to the tenth day. They are sprayed quite thoroughly, some men using water enough so that it runs out of the bottom of the machine. No particular care is taken to see that the water used is warm. Ordinary water just as it comes from the pipes is commonly used and is applied by means of a spray nozzle attached to a hose. However, extremely cold water should not be used for this purpose. This spraying is done once or twice a day as the operator may think necessary until the eggs begin to hatch. In many cases even then if the ducklings seem to be drying too fast after they come out of the shell, or to be having difficulty to get out it is well to open the machines and wet the eggs down thoroughly.

Fertility. The fertility varies with the season that is, with the weather. At the beginning of the laying season when the weather is cold the fertility usually runs rather low. This is likewise true at the end of the laying season when the heat of summer sets in. During the interval between these two times of low fertility there will usually be one or more periods during which the fertility will go down and then come back again. This seems to occur even though the weather remains about the same and though there is no change in the method of feeding. Fertility may be considered to be good when it runs about 85%. When the fertility is running poor the hatching of the eggs left in the machines after testing will usually be poor also.

Hatching. It takes longer as a rule from the time that the ducklings pip the eggs until they hatch than it does with chicks. To retain the moisture which is so necessary during hatching, the machines are usually shut tightly and are not opened until the hatching is pretty well completed unless it becomes necessary to add more moisture as indicated above. The little ducklings should be left in the incubator until the hatching is over and they are thoroughly dried off. As soon as the hatching is completed, the ventilators in the machines are opened to hasten the drying process. If the ducklings open their bills and pant it is an indication that they are not getting enough ventilation and this should be supplied by fastening the machine door open a little way. If the ducks are not ready to be taken out of the machines by noon or soon after, it is best to leave them until the next morning before removing them to the brooder house. In the meantime, however, the old eggs and shells and other refuse should be taken out. Usually the hatch is completed in time so that the ducklings can be removed to the brooder house on the afternoon of the 28th day. As a rule the earlier the hatch is completed the better are the ducklings.

Figures secured on results in hatching for the entire season on Long Island duck farms indicate that as a whole the duck raisers will not average much over 40% hatch of all eggs set. Some hatches may run as high as 60% or even more and in some seasons the average percentage will run higher than 40. Some especially skilled operators may also secure considerably better average results than this. It is quite a common practice on the part of duck farmers to pay their incubator man a bonus on all ducklings over 40% hatched during the season. This bonus may range anywhere from $1 to $5 per thousand ducklings. Such an arrangement serves to give the incubator man a greater incentive to give the machines good attention and to secure just the best results of which he is capable.

Selling Baby Ducks. Within the last two or three years there has sprung into existence a small but increasing trade in baby ducks. They are handled and shipped about the same as baby chicks. Baby ducks are ready for shipment as soon as they are thoroughly dry, usually about 12 hours after the hatch starts to come off. They are neither fed nor watered before shipment and are packed in cardboard boxes used in shipping baby chicks. As a rule the shipping boxes will accommodate about half the number of ducklings that they will chicks. Of course the outside temperature very largely governs the matter of the number to a compartment. In warm summer weather, a two compartment box intended for 50 chicks will accommodate 26 ducklings if well ventilated at the sides and top. They are shipped by parcel post and can be sent anywhere within a radius of one thousand miles if the trip does not require more than 36 hours. For best results the ducklings should not be allowed to go much beyond this length of time before they are fed. On receipt they should be placed immediately in a brooder already prepared for them.

CHAPTER VI

Commercial Duck Farming--Brooding and Rearing the Young Stock

Young ducks are easier to brood than chicks. They seem to learn more quickly where the source of heat is and they are less likely to cause trouble from crowding. They are also less subject to disease.

Removing the Newly Hatched Ducklings to the Brooder House. The ducklings should be left in the incubator until they are thoroughly dried off. Usually they will be dried so that they can be moved on the afternoon of the 28th day of incubation. If, however, they are not ready early in the afternoon it is best to leave them in the machine until the next morning. In moving the ducklings, place them in boxes, baskets or other suitable carriers and cover them with burlap or cloth to avoid any danger of the ducklings becoming chilled.

Brooder Houses Repaired. There are many different types and styles of brooder houses which are used with success. For this reason only one type of each class of brooder house needed is described in detail. These particular houses have been in successful use for a considerable period of time and are given because they embody all the necessary requisites for such houses and at the same time utilize the space to good advantage and are economical in construction.

In general there are required three different brooder houses. The first of these requires sufficient heating capacity so that the temperature of the house itself can be maintained at 65 to 70 degrees even in the cold weather of winter or early spring. In addition, hovers are required in this house under which a temperature can be maintained from 80 to 90 degrees. For convenience this house will be spoken of as brooder house No. 1. A second brooder house which can be called brooder house No. 2 will be required which is equipped with heating apparatus so that the temperature can be run up to 60 degrees when required. The third brooder house known as brooder house No. 3 is a cold brooder house or one without artificial heat. It furnishes shelter for the young ducks where they can be driven in at night and during the day in cold weather. As the ducklings pass out of the brooder house No. 3 they are housed in sheds or shelters with yards which usually extend into the water but which may not do so in all cases.

Brooder House No. 1

The length of this house determines its capacity, the required amount of which will depend upon the output of any particular plant. There should be brooder capacity in this house sufficient to care for approximately ?of the total output for the year at one time.

Construction of House. A suitable house which has been in practical use for some time consists of one 20 feet wide and running east and west with windows in the south or front side. If the location were right such a house could be run north and south to good advantage and should then have windows on each side so as to let in the sunlight from both directions. The front wall of this house is 7 feet high, the back wall 4 feet. The ridge of the house is about 2 feet in front of the center, the front slope of the roof having an eight inch pitch while the back slope has a 6 inch pitch. The roof rafters are 2 ?4's placed every two feet. The studs and plates are likewise 2 ?4. The walls are made of matched material. The roof is constructed of 1 ?2 inch strips placed every 4 inches and these covered with shingles. Tie beams every 8 feet extend from front to rear plates. This particular brooder house is not ceiled but a good tight ceiling 8 feet above the walk or runway would make it easier to keep the house clean and would also render it somewhat easier in cold weather to maintain the temperature desired. The house is built on a concrete wall or foundation and a dirt floor is used but the dirt must be filled in well above the level of the ground outside so that there is no danger of water coming into the house or the floors becoming damp or sloppy. Windows are placed in the front wall, one to each pen. In every other pen there is a small door in the back of the house to facilitate cleaning out the pens. A window can be substituted for this door to good advantage as it makes the house lighter.

Heating Apparatus. Heat is furnished by means of a coal burning stove which heats water and causes it to circulate through pipes run the length of the house. The heater must always be placed in the windward end of the building as otherwise it is hard to get the heat down to the other end as the wind tends to drive it back. The hot water pipes are carried down the center of the house and the return pipes are located in the same place. A low partition is run lengthwise of the house dividing the pipes and thus forming double pens, half extending from the center to the front and half from the center to the rear of the house. The pipes and the partition between them is covered over with boards making a 4 foot walk or runway directly over the pipes, which comes into most convenient use as a place to convey, by means of a wheelbarrow, feed or other material needed in the house, and as a convenient place from which to care for the ducklings in the pens on each side. This board covering over the pipes also serves to hold the heat and thus forms hovers.

It is advisable to partition off the first third of the house, that is, the portion in which the heater is located, with a solid partition. Then by having suitable valves in the pipes, the heat can be cut off from the rest of the house and only the smaller partitioned off end used as a separate and independent section of the brooder. This is especially useful when only a small number of ducklings are being hatched early in the spring when the weather is cold and it may be difficult to heat the whole building properly. It is also economical in fuel under such conditions.

If, on the other hand, the number of ducklings hatched during the cold weather is so large that all or nearly all of the house capacity is needed to care for them, it will usually pay to install an additional heater, the pipes from which can be run along the rear wall of the building, in order to keep up a proper house temperature when the weather is severe.

Pens. Having the hovers in the center of the house, makes it possible to have double sets of pens, one running from the center to the front wall and the other from the center to the rear wall. The pens are divided off by means of partitions made of one foot boards. These are high enough to confine the ducklings to their own pen and at the same time are easy to step over. In a house of this width, 20 feet, with 4 feet in the center taken up by the double hovers or walk, each pen is 8 feet long in the clear or 10 feet to the partition under the hover. The pens in the first third of the house are made 5 feet wide, in the next third 6 feet and in the last third 7 feet wide. When the ducklings are first brought from the incubator cellar they are placed in the pens nearest the heater as the temperature will run somewhat higher there than in the portions of the house more remote from the heater. These 5 ?10 foot pens will accommodate 125 baby ducklings although better results will be obtained by placing only 100 in a pen if sufficient room is available. Some duck growers use boards which can be slipped into slots made of cleats nailed to the pen partitions at different distances from the hover and which serve to confine the baby ducklings close to the hover for the first few days or until they learn to go under the hover to get warm.

As additional ducklings are hatched later and brought to the brooder house, the ducklings already there are moved along the necessary number of pens in order to accommodate the new-comers in the pens nearest the heater. For this purpose, a small door is made in each partition next the outside wall of the house through which the ducklings can be driven. A broom is a handy implement to use in driving the ducklings as they can be pushed along in front of it. It is best to drive the ducklings just after they have been fed as they are not so nervous and afraid at that time.

The increased width of the pens in the second and third portions of the house is for the purpose of taking care of the growth of the ducklings as they are moved along the house. Pens of the same width as those in which they were started become too crowded as the ducklings increase in size.

Equipment of the Pen. The equipment of the pens is quite simple. Water is piped through the house along both walls so that it is available to each pen. A spigot is provided in each pen and under this is placed the drinking dish, which consists of a round metal pan about a foot in diameter and 3 or 4 inches deep. A square pan should never be used as the ducklings are apt to get their bills caught in the corners. One quarter inch mesh wire netting is bent in a circle and placed in the drinking dish as a guard to keep the ducklings from getting into the pan. This guard should be made of such size that there is a space between the wire and the edge of the dish of about 1?inches all around. This guard should be about 8 inches high. The water pan itself is set upon a wire covered frame about 18 inches square under which is dug a pit 4 or 5 inches deep to drain away any water which the ducklings slop out of the pan. Such an arrangement keeps the pens from becoming sloppy and damp.

Each pen must also have a flat metal dish on which to place the feed for the little ducks. Metal pans are better than wooden feeding trays as they are easier to keep clean.

In each pen is provided a small hopper filled with fine sharp creek sand to which the ducklings have access at all times. Some duck growers prefer to mix the sand in the feed rather than to provide it in hoppers. After the ducklings are allowed to run in the yards, sand need not be furnished if the yards are sand as the ducklings will help themselves. If the land in the yards is not sand, however, it is necessary to continue to furnish this material.

Grading and Sorting the Ducklings. As the ducklings are moved from pen to pen through this house as well as the other houses, they are constantly graded for size and thriftiness, the smaller, less thrifty individuals being left with younger lots. Some ducklings do not grow as quickly as others, and these if left with ducklings larger than themselves will not get their share of the feed and will not do as well. In this connection it should be noted that when young ducks are not fairly clean it is a good indication that they are not doing as well as they should.

Cleaning and Bedding the Pens. Careful attention must be given to keeping the pens and the ducklings themselves clean if they are to do well. Therefore the pens must be cleaned out as often as may be necessary to accomplish this purpose. The judgment of the brooder man must decide how often this is necessary but it will be at least once a week. When cleaning the pens the old bedding is thrown out from the front pens through the windows and from the back pens through the door provided in the rear wall for this purpose. Bedding the pens must be done more frequently, usually about every other day. Fresh bedding will help to absorb the droppings and will keep the pens from becoming sloppy or sticky. For bedding, straw, meadow hay, swale hay or any other suitable material available should be utilized.

Ventilation. Plenty of ventilation is required in the brooder house in order to take out the ammonia odor which arises from the droppings. Properly managed, the doors and windows provide sufficient means of ventilation but some duck growers prefer to have roof ventilators in addition.

Other Types of Brooder Houses. Many other types of brooder houses are used, some of them being shed roof construction and many of them being built narrower than this house, that is to say, 14, 16 or 18 feet wide with an alleyway along the front or rear side of the house from which the work is done. The hovers are placed at the back of the pens when the alley-way is in the front, otherwise, they are placed next to the alley-way. The disadvantages of these houses are that only single pens are provided and that valuable brooding space is used up by the alley-way. The advantages of the house described above lie in the fact that the hovers are in the center of the house with the pens on each side of this, thus doubling the capacity, and that by making use of a walk over the hover pipe no room is wasted in an alley-way. Having pens on each side also lessens the labor of taking care of the ducklings to some extent as the arrangement is more compact.

Length of Time in Brooder

In House No. 1. As a rule the ducklings are kept in the No. 1 house until they are from 2 to 3 weeks old, this of course depending somewhat upon the time of year and the weather and also upon the number of ducklings for which accommodations must be provided at any particular time. As the ducks are moved down through the house and eventually reach the last pens they are taken from this house and placed in brooder house No. 2.

Brooder House No. 2. This is a heated house like brooder house No. 1 but in which it is not necessary to maintain so high a temperature. Sufficient heating apparatus should be installed to make it possible to maintain the temperature at 60 degrees if this becomes necessary in the early spring.

The particular brooder house described is 14 feet wide and has a shed roof. It is provided with a window in the front of each pen. No openings are required along the back since this is not a double pen house. The space in such a house could undoubtedly be used to better advantage if it were constructed as wide as the No. 1 house and the hot water pipes and walk put through the middle of the house so as to provide double pens. In this house the hot water pipes are run along the rear of the pens, and while hovers are not really necessary, a walk is constructed over the pipes in order to save space and provide a convenient place from which to do the work, and this forms hovers.

Ordinarily after May 1 no heat is needed in the No. 2 house. The pens in this house are 12 feet wide and they are equipped with feeding and watering arrangements as in brooder house No. 1. As the ducklings are moved to this house from the No. 1 house from 150 to 200 are placed in each pen. They are moved through the house from pen to pen in the same manner as in the No. 1 house to make way for new arrivals. As a rule they stay in this house about two weeks depending somewhat on the weather and upon the number of ducklings being brooded. Yards are used in connection with this house which are the same width as the pens and 50 feet in length. As in the No. 1 house the pens in this house should be cleaned at least once a week and they should be bedded with straw or other bedding material every other day. As soon as the ducks have been moved through this No. 2 house they are put in brooder house No. 3.

Brooder House No. 3

This is a shed roof house 16 feet wide equipped with single pens. No heat is required in this house. Yards of the same width as the pens and 50 feet deep are used. Usually the ducks are fed outside the house from a wagon driven along a roadway just in front of the yards.

The pens are 16 feet wide and the same number of ducks is used in them as in the No. 2 house. As a rule the ducks stay in this house about 2 weeks and are then moved to the duck pens or shelters with the larger yards which may or may not have water. From this point on the ducks are termed yard ducks.

In all three of the brooder houses the young ducks are supplied with their drinking water from pipes through the houses. They are not given access to water until they are moved to the yards.

Yard Accommodations for Ducklings

As the ducklings get to be 8 weeks old they can stand ordinary weather conditions and it is not absolutely necessary to have houses for them. However, it is common and good practice to provide shelter where they can be housed at night and can take refuge from storms. A suitable house for this purpose consists of a building 16 ?24 feet divided into two parts with 200 ducklings to a side. This house is 5 feet high in front and 3?feet in back. It is set on posts with a baseboard around it to make it tight. It can be constructed of matched stuff or unmatched stuff covered with paper. The front is left open but curtains are placed on the front which can be used to close the openings so as to keep out the snow. These are used only in the winter. When the ducklings are first started in these sheds they are shut in when desired by means of wire panels fitted into the lower part of the open front. The ducklings are left in these yards and fed there until they are ready for market.

Shade. Shade is important for the ducklings as soon as the sun gets hot.

Exposure to the sun without shade will cause quite a heavy loss in ducklings. If natural shade is not furnished by trees, some artificial means must be adopted to supply the shade. This may take the form of shelters or low frames covered with boards, brush or burlap.

Feeding. The first feed and water is given as soon as the ducks are placed in the No. 1 brooder house or when 24 to 36 hours old. They are fed 3 times a day, in the morning about 6 a. m., at noon, and at night about 4:30 or 5 o'clock. The time of feeding should be regular, and fairly early in the morning but not any earlier in the afternoon than one can help so that the time between the evening and the morning feed will not be too long. Some growers prefer to feed 4 or 5 times daily for the first week or two. The birds are fed as much as they will clean up at each feeding and if any feed is left it should be gathered up so that it will not sour and cause digestive troubles.

The first feed consists of the following:--One measure corn meal, one measure bran, one measure ground crackers, stale bread or shredded wheat waste, one measure in 10 of beef scrap or fish, one measure in 6 of creek grass or other very fine green stuff. Green rye or oats should never be used for this purpose after it becomes jointed. If the feed is mixed up with cold water about ?measure of low-grade wheat flour should be used to cause it to stick together. If hot water is used in the mixing this is not needed.

Sand must be fed either by mixing it in to the extent of about 3% of the ration or the sand can be fed separately in hoppers as previously described. This same mixture may be fed in the No. 1, No. 2, and No. 3 brooder houses, or in other words, until ducklings go to the yards, or ration No. 2 given below may be substituted either at the start or after a week or ten days. After the ducklings go to the yards the following fattening ration is used: 200 pounds corn meal, 100 pounds low-grade flour, 100 pounds bran, 1 part in 10 of beef scrap and 2 tubs or bushels of green stuff. Some duck growers prefer to feed 300 pounds of corn meal instead of 200 pounds. This ration like the other is fed 3 times a day. Of course, there are many different rations in use with good results, every grower having more or less personal preferences in this matter. A proper proportion of animal feed, consisting of beef scrap or fish is very important as the ducklings will not grow and make normal gains if this is omitted or reduced in amount.

Much has been written about the feeding of celery seed to fattening ducklings for the purpose of improving the flavor of the flesh and formerly ducklings were advertised and sold as "celery-fed". As a matter of fact, the amount of celery seed fed was small and it is questionable how much influence it had on the flavor of the birds. At the present time, celery seed is not used in fattening the ducklings on most of the large duck farms of Long Island.

A comparison of gains made by ducklings on two different rations is shown in the following table. Ration No. 1 consists of the fattening ration given above. Ration No. 2 consists of 100 pounds bran, 100 pounds corn meal, 50 pounds rolled oats, 50 pounds gluten feed, 10% beef scrap. The ducks used were three days old at the first weighing and there were 27 in each lot. After the second weighing the number in each lot was reduced to 24 ducks.

	Feed No. 1		Feed No. 2	
	Total Weight	Average Weight	Total Weight	Average Wt
August 14	4?lbs.	0.176	4?lbs.	0.176
August 21	10 "	0.37	9?"	0.352
August 28	16?"	0.687	17?"	0.729
September 5	25 "	1.041	27 "	1.125
September 13	44?"	1.854	48?"	2.02
September 19	50 "	2.083	56?"	2.354
September 27	64 "	2.666	67 "	2.62
October 4	78?"	3.27	82?"	3.437
October 11	99?"	4.145	103?"	4.312
October 18	115?"	4.812	119 "	4.958
October 25	126 "	5.25	135 "	5.62

Lights for Ducklings. Often when the ducks are about one-third grown or about 4 weeks old they will stampede at night at any unusual noise or any other disturbance. In doing this, especially when they are in fairly large lots, they surge back and forth in the pens, running over one another with the result that their backs are torn and scratched while not infrequently more serious injuries result and may cause cripples. To keep them quiet it is common to use lights at night. Formerly lanterns were used but now on most duck plants electric lights are available for this purpose. For a house 140 feet long, six 15-watt lights scattered at equal intervals will be sufficient, and these can be used in like proportion for houses of other lengths. The lights are left on all night. Even when the ducks are half grown and may be out on the yards it is still necessary to use lights on stormy nights so that they will stay in and keep quiet and not get drowned in the rain. With a 16 ?24 foot house such as described previously, a single 25 watt light is sufficient. Ducklings are especially likely to be stampeded during thunderstorms and if a storm is coming up it is well to turn on the lights and to shut the ducklings in their shelters when they are first placed in the yards. One should not carry a lantern when moving among the ducklings at night as this will cause moving shadows which are very likely to frighten and stampede the birds.

Pounds of Feed to Produce a Pound of Market Duck. It is stated by long established duck growers that from 5 to 7 pounds of feed is required, this including the feed given to the breeding ducks for the season, to produce a pound of market duck.

Water for Young Ducks. Drinking water is provided to the ducklings while in the brooder houses by means of a piped supply. The drinking pans are filled at each feeding time but at no other time. Water is not left before them continuously while they are in the brooder houses as they would be working in it all the time and this would keep them dirty and make the house sloppy. After they are put out on the yards they may or may not be provided with water in which they can swim. Most duck growers on Long Island allow them to have access to water. While it is undoubtedly true that swimming in the water induces them to take more exercise and thus tends to reduce somewhat the rapidity of fattening, at the same time it lessens the labor very materially as they do not need to be provided with a supply of drinking water other than the water in which they swim. Ducklings can be grown very successfully with only a limited amount of water, that is, only enough to drink and in which to wash themselves.

Age and Weight When Ready for Market. Ducklings are usually marketed when they are 10 to 12 weeks old. A partial moult on the neck and breast occurs about this time giving them a somewhat rough look. This indicates that they are in proper condition to kill. If killing is not done within a week after this moult starts they will begin to lose flesh and it will be some time before they will fatten again. Ducks when ready to ship will average from 5 to 6 pounds. A majority will weigh nearer 5 than 6 pounds. A pen of fattened ducks is driven up to the killing house and into a pen where each one is caught up and examined to see if it is in good condition. If the duck has a good smooth breast so that the breastbone is not felt when handled and is well fleshed on the back it is ready to kill. If it is not in this condition it is thrown out and these thin ducks are returned to the yards for further fattening or are utilized for shipping alive. Thin ducks are generally used for live shipments as they will not shrink as much as well fattened ducks.

[Illustration: FIG. 35. An important part of rations for ducks. Green feed ready to be cut up into short lengths suitable for mixing in the feed. (Photograph from the Bureau of Animal Industry, U. S. Department of Agriculture.)]

[Illustration: FIG. 36. Feeding fattening or yard ducks from the feeding track. (Photograph from the Bureau of Animal Industry, U. S. Department of Agriculture.)]

Cripples. There will always be found in the flocks more or less crippled ducks and those with crooked backs, twisted wings, etc. As a rule ducks with twisted wings fatten well and are in good condition and can be killed about as soon as any of the others. The crippled ducks are sorted out into a lot by themselves where they are held until they can be put into condition to market. It is doubtful whether it pays the duck growers to bother with these ducks since they are rather difficult to condition and it would probably pay better to kill them. However, it is quite common practice to carry them until they can be marketed.

Cleaning the Yards. The yards must be cleaned whenever they need it. It is a matter of judgment to decide when this is necessary but they must be cleaned whenever they get sticky or sloppy. The weather will have a considerable influence upon the frequency of cleaning which may be necessary once in two weeks, or in the yards of brooder houses Nos. 2 and 3 may run as often as once a week. In dry weather the yards are cleaned by sweeping up the droppings and carting them away. In wet weather the ducks in running about over the yard pack down the droppings until they form a sort of putty-like layer which has to be scraped off with a hoe.

Critical Period with Young Ducks. The critical period with young ducks is the first week of their existence. With good management after they have passed this point not many are lost. The loss in young ducks from the time they are hatched until they are ready for market will range all the way from 5 to 30%. When the loss does not average more than 10% for the season this is considered good. Undoubtedly many duck raisers lose a greater percent than 10.

[Illustration: FIG. 37. Yard ducks at rest. (Photograph from the Bureau of

Animal Industry. U. S. Department of Agriculture.)]

[Illustration: FIG. 38. On this plant, the lay of the land was such that not all of the yards could be run down to the stream. So a shallow canal was dug from the stream through the yards which were without natural water frontage. (Photograph from the Bureau of Animal Industry, U. S. Department of Agriculture.)]

Disease Prevention

Trouble from disease in young ducks is not severe although there is a greater loss from this source than in the case of mature ducks. The aim of the grower should be to use such methods of management and feeding as will keep the ducklings in good health and reduce the losses to a minimum. To accomplish this care must be taken to see that the brooding temperatures are correct, that the feed used contains what the ducklings need, that they are not overfed and that the house and yards are clean and dry and the feed and water dishes are clean. Remember that green feed and animal feed are essential ingredients in the ration.

Gapes or Pneumonia. One of the principal troubles is a disease which is called "pneumonia" by some duck raisers and by others "gapes". It is not the same disease which is called gapes in chickens. In fact, it is a form of cold which approaches pneumonia. The little ducks stretch their necks up and breathe hard and usually die within a comparatively short time. This disease may affect either the baby ducks or ducks which are old enough to kill. All that can be done is to make sure that the housing and brooding conditions are such as to correct the trouble which causes the colds.

Fits. In addition, the little ducks for the first 3 or 4 days may be more or less subject to a disease which is called "fits" by some duck growers. With this disease they simply keel over and soon die. It is probably a digestive difficulty of some sort. The feeding of plenty of green stuff or the turning of the ducks out on grass will usually stop this trouble.

Diarrhoea. This is a fairly common trouble. It may be due to improper feeding, or to too high or low temperature in the brooder. The obvious treatment is to remedy the cause or causes of the trouble.

Lameness. Not infrequently growers, particularly beginners, experience difficulty from a fairly large proportion of their ducklings becoming lame. This may grow worse until a considerable number of the birds will die. This trouble may be due to a lack of animal matter and mineral matter in the ration or may be due to digestive troubles caused by poor rations, by over feeding, by failing to gather up feed not eaten by the ducklings and leaving it to sour, or by lack of cleanliness of the feed and water dishes. Where the pens are allowed to become damp and sloppy this may also cause some lameness.

Sore Eyes. Occasionally duck growers complain that their ducklings suffer from sore eyes. This may be due to a cold causing a discharge from the eyes or may be due to the use of too sloppy feed which adheres to the eyes and causes an irritation. Affected birds should be placed in a separate pen from the others and the eyes should be bathed with an antiseptic solution.

Feather Eating or "Quilling". This is a bad habit which is apt to cause more or less trouble when the ducklings are about two-thirds grown. It is much more likely to occur when the birds are kept in cramped quarters. It is usually started by one or a few individuals but when the feathers are injured so that they begin to bleed, which they will very quickly do, the vice will spread among the whole flock and serious damage will occur. It is therefore necessary to be on the lookout for this trouble, and as soon as detected, the birds responsible should be removed. If the culprits are placed with older birds which are already feathered, they will not trouble by trying to eat the feathers. It is the blood in the growing feathers which attracts them. If the habit has become general, it is more difficult to check. About the best thing that can be done, is to turn them out in a roomy yard, one with a growing green crop, if available, where they will be so busy as to stop the feather eating of their own accord.

Rats.--Rats are very destructive if they get into the brooder house. A single rat has been known to kill and drag off as many as 200 ducklings in one night. If a rat gets into the brooder house it is therefore of the utmost importance that it be hunted down and killed without delay. Otherwise serious losses will result.

Cooperative Feed Association

A very large proportion of the feed used on a duck plant is that which is fed to the market ducks. By purchasing feed in considerable quantities the duck grower is able to cut down the cost to some extent. A number of the duck raisers on Long Island have developed this idea further by forming a cooperative feed organization. Stock in this concern is held both by the duck growers and by outsiders but is controlled by the duck growers. The feed association maintains a feed warehouse, purchases feeds in quantity and does business both with the duck growers and with other persons in the market for feed. The existence of a cooperative feed purchasing association of this sort not only cuts down to some extent the cost of feed but likewise makes it possible for the duck growers to have greater assurance of securing the supply which is so necessary to them during the growing season.

CHAPTER VII

Commercial Duck Farming--Marketing

On commercial duck farms, the business consists mainly of producing large quickly grown ducklings which are marketed before they are mature. Because of this immaturity, the ducks are quite commonly termed green ducks. The business has also become so highly specialized on Long Island and this is such a center of the industry, that the birds are commonly quoted on the New York market as Long Island ducklings.

Proper Age to Market. It is important that the ducklings be marketed as soon as they have reached the proper age and stage of development. When the ducklings are about 10 to 12 weeks old they begin to shed their first growth of feathers. This is apparent first on the neck and breast, giving them somewhat of a rough appearance. The ducklings must be marketed within one week after they begin this moult. If they are allowed to go longer than this they will begin to get thin and as it will take them 6 weeks or more to grow a new crop of feathers it will be a considerable period before they get back in market condition again and any additional weight which they may attain will not be sufficient to pay for the feed eaten during this period.

Weights at the Time of Marketing. Well grown ducklings should average in weight from 5 to 6 pounds at 10 to 12 weeks of age when they are ready to be marketed. A majority of the ducks will weigh closer to 5 pounds than they will to 6. The vast majority of ducklings are marketed at this age as it does not pay to keep them past the time they reach prime market condition. On commercial duck farms practically the only ducks which are marketed at an older age than this are the breeders which are turned off at the end of the laying season and the ducklings which by reason of their being crippled or less thrifty are not in suitable market condition at this time and are held longer until they are in good condition. The ducklings are marketed from early spring until late fall. The time at which ducklings are first available for market in any quantity depends upon the earliness with which the breeders begin to lay and the end of the season depends upon how late the breeders continue to lay at a profitable rate.

The Last Feed for Market Ducks. It is important in order to have the dressed ducklings appear to the best advantage and also in order to insure their keeping qualities as much as possible that they should have no feed in their crops when they are killed. This means that if they are to be killed in the morning, which is the usual practice, they should be fed for the last time the previous night. If, however, they are not to be killed until afternoon they can be fed lightly in the morning.

Sorting Market Ducklings. When a pen of ducklings which are being fattened are deemed ready to be killed they are driven up to the killing house and a few of them at a time driven into a small pen where it is easy to catch and examine them. Each duck as it is caught is examined to make sure that it is in proper market condition. The examination consists of feeling of the duck's body to see that it has a good smooth breast so that the breast bone cannot be readily felt. If it is in that condition it is ready to kill. Ducks which do not show this condition are thrown out and returned to the yards where they are fed for a longer period unless it is desired to ship them alive.

At the proper season of the year when breeders for the next season are to be selected, suitable birds for that purpose are picked out from the market lots as they are examined. In any lot of ducks there will be found some cripples. It is common practice to sort these out and group them together in a pen by themselves where they are held until they are in suitable condition for marketing. It is doubtful whether it pays to hold these cripples as they are hard to get in good condition and in many cases are probably kept and fed at a loss. Some ducklings will show twisted wings but as a rule they are thrifty and will fatten readily and be in good market condition.

Killing. As the ducklings suitable for killing are selected, 10 or 12 of them, depending upon the capacity of the killing room, are hung up by their feet, the head being fastened down by means of a hook or else weighted down by means of a blood can hung from a hook inserted through the bill. By means of a long, narrow bladed sharp knife the veins in the throat just beyond the skull are severed so as to cause free bleeding. The blood flows either into the blood can or into a trough above which the birds are hung. The birds are not stuck or brained unless it is desired to dry pick them nor are they as a rule stunned by hitting them on the head before bleeding. In some states, however, the law requires that all birds bled shall first be stunned in this manner. The bleeding of the ducks causes their death and they are allowed to hang until they are thoroughly bled out. They are then taken down, the blood washed off of their heads and placed on a table or on the floor convenient to the pickers, other ducks being hung in their places.

Scalding. The picker selects a duck from the table where they are placed after being taken down and carries it to a large kettle of water which is maintained at a temperature just below boiling. They are thoroughly soused in this water holding them by the head and feet so as to allow the water to penetrate into the feathers until they can be readily plucked. The picker tests the readiness with which the feathers come out by plucking a few from the breast or body and thus determines whether the scalding is sufficient or whether more is required. Care is taken not to dip the feet or head in the water as this might discolor these parts. Practically all market ducks from Long Island are scald picked at the present time. Dry picking which is demanded in some markets such as Boston makes a somewhat better looking carcass and also increases the value of the feathers, but is generally considered too slow and too highly skilled a process for use on the average duck farm.

Picking.. After scalding the picker starts removing the feathers. In doing this the duck is held either on the lap or on a board nailed to the side of the feather box. The feathers on the breast are picked first, then working down toward the tail, pulling the feathers with the grain. The soft body feathers as plucked are thrown into the feather box, the coarser feathers being thrown on the floor. The main wing and tail feathers are left on as are likewise some of the feathers of the neck next the head.

The most troublesome part of picking ducks is removing the down. This may be removed to some extent by rubbing with the hand although care must be taken not to bruise the skin severely. In some cases the down is shaved off with a sharp knife. In some of the commercial packing houses the duck's body is sprinkled with powdered rosin and then dipped into the hot water. This melts the rosin so that the down and rosin can be rubbed off easily with the hand leaving the body clean. Pin feathers are usually removed by grasping them between the thumb and a dull knife.

In some packing houses, ducks are steamed before picking. Where this is done they are picked clean and the wing and tail feathers are pulled before steaming takes place. Six or eight ducks which have been bled are hung at the same time in the top of a steam box or barrel which can be made air-tight and the steam turned on until the soft feathers of the breast come off easily. The length of time to steam depends on the temperature of the steam itself and varies from one-half to 2 minutes. In some cases the ducks are hung in a steam box with the heads outside so as to prevent the steam from coming into contact with the heads, possibly discoloring them.

On Long Island women are used very largely for picking and they secure for this service 6 cents per duck. A good picker should do 75 ducks or even more a day. The value of the feathers will slightly more than pay for the cost of picking.

Picking usually begins early in the morning about 6 o'clock and is generally finished by noon or soon after. Most duck raisers figure on doing their killing and picking during the first half of the week and do not like to kill if they can help it during the latter days of the week.

[Illustration: FIG. 46. Picking the ducks. (Photograph from the Bureau of Animal Industry, U. S. Department of Agriculture.)]

Dry Picking. Where the market requires it, the ducks must be dry picked. In doing this the procedure is the same as in dry picking chickens. After the cut is made to bleed the ducks, the point of the knife is plunged through the roof of the mouth until it reaches the brain when it is turned to cause a paralysis of the muscles which enables the feathers to be plucked more easily. The duck is then struck on the back of the head with a club to stun it and make it easier to handle when picking. The picker seats himself by the feather box, with the duck on his lap, holding the head pressed against the outside of the box and held there by the picker's leg. He then proceeds immediately and as quickly as possible to pluck the feathers. It is necessary to accomplish this without delay, for the feathers soon set and are then much harder to pluck and are more likely to result in tears in the skin. When removing the down, the hand is moistened when much of the down can be rubbed off. Pin feathers are removed by grasping them between the thumb and the edge of a dull knife and any which cannot be gotten in this way are shaved off with a sharp knife. After picking, the carcasses are cooled in cold water the same as the scalded birds.

Cooling. After the birds are plucked they are thrown into cold water and are left there for several hours or until the body heat is entirely removed. It is most important that this be thoroughly accomplished for if any body heat is left in the carcasses they are almost sure to become green-struck when packed. The length of time that they must be left in the water depends upon the weather conditions. If the weather is warm so that the water is not very cool it is necessary to add ice in order to hasten the cooling and to accomplish it thoroughly. Cooling in water also serves to plump the carcasses somewhat.

Packing. After the ducks are thoroughly cooled they are removed from the water and packed. Long Island ducklings are usually packed in barrels. Forty-five ducks will pack in a sugar barrel and 33 in a flour barrel. The proper number for the barrel used is placed on hanging spring scales and weighed before being packed. The best method of packing is to lay the ducks on their sides. If they are packed on their backs or bellies, the ice used between the layers is apt to cause a cutting or bruising of the soft abdomens and injure the appearance of the carcasses. Between each layer of ducks a scoopful of cracked ice is used although in cool weather it may only be necessary to use half a scoop of ice. After the barrel is packed it should be allowed to stand for a while to settle. Then the top of the barrel is piled up with cracked ice and covered with burlap. On the side of the barrel is marked the number of ducks and their weight. Later a card is tacked alongside of this showing the consignee's and the shipper's names as well as the number of ducks and their weight.

Shipping. The barrels should be packed and shipped the same evening. Shipping may be done either by express or by automobile truck. A good many of the Long Island ducklings are now shipped into New York City by truck.

Cooperative Marketing Association. The duck growers on Long Island have formed a cooperative marketing association. This association maintains its own house in New York City and sells practically the entire output of Long Island ducklings, controlling probably 90%. During the year 1919 there were in the neighborhood of 800,000 head of ducks marketed through this house. Practically all of the capital stock of this concern is held by the duck growers and they are not allowed to sell any of their stock without first offering it to the association.

Prices for Ducks. Early in the season the ducklings bring the best prices, that is to say from March 1 to May 1. Then as the output of ducks increases prices gradually drop. The heaviest shipments occur in June, July and August. In September as the output of ducks begins to drop off the price begins to climb a little. The following prices as quoted in the New York Produce Review show the range from March, 1920, to June, 1921.

Shipping Ducks Alive. While the great majority of ducks are shipped dressed there is some shipment of live ducks. This is particularly true during the Jewish holidays in March and in September and October when the demand for live ducks and the price paid for them is excellent. As a rule it pays better to ship alive the ducks which are inclined to be a little thin rather than to ship those which are in top market condition. This is due to the fact that fat ducks will shrink very considerably when cooped and shipped alive, this shrinkage running from one-half to three-quarters of a pound per head where they are cooped not to exceed 12 to 15 hours. The ducks which are in the fattest condition will shrink the most. At the season of the year when live ducks are in best demand it often pays to ship alive the ducklings which are sorted out as not being in the best condition rather than to hold them for further fattening.

Saving the Feathers. The feathers from the ducks form quite an important source of revenue to the duck farmers. As stated before the value of the feathers will a little more than pay for the cost of picking and since this is a considerable item of expense the grower cannot afford to neglect the feathers. The soft body feathers are kept separate from the coarser feathers, the latter being thrown on the floor as they are plucked. These coarser feathers are later swept up and are commonly spoken of as sweepings. Feathers from dry-picked ducks are superior in quality and bring a better price but most of the duck feathers now marketed from commercial duck farms are scalded feathers. The feathers after each day's killing are gathered up and spread out in a loft where they can be placed in a layer not over 3 or 4 inches deep. This should be an airy place so as to give the feathers a good place to dry out. On the second day they are scraped up in a pile and then spread out again, thus turning them over and changing their position. They are then left until they are dry enough to sack which should be in a little over a week. Unless the feathers are thoroughly dried out they will heat when sacked and this will seriously hurt their market quality. When dry they are packed either in the large special feather sacks made for this purpose or in smaller sacks, about as big as two bran sacks, which will hold from 60 to 80 pounds of feathers. The feathers are shipped to regular feather dealers or manufacturers.

[Illustration: FIG. 49. A valuable by-product of duck plants. The feathers from a duck will pay for the cost of picking. (Photograph from the Bureau of Animal Industry, U. S. Department of Agriculture.)]

Prices and Uses of Duck Feathers. The soft body feathers and the coarser feathers often called "sweepings" should be kept and sold separate. While scalded feathers are not worth as much as dry picked feathers, the former if properly dried out or cured will find a ready sale. Feathers packed before they are thoroughly dried out, are likely to arrive at their destination in a matted and musty or heated condition. This, of course, injures their quality and the price paid for them is discounted according to their condition.

The soft body feathers of ducks are used almost entirely for bedding purposes, that is, are put in pillows and feather beds. White feathers are preferred and usually bring a somewhat higher price.

The prices paid for the feathers vary quite widely at different times of the year, and in different sections of the country, and also of course with the condition of the feathers themselves. The quotations given below represent the prices paid in June, 1921.

Duck Feathers Cents Per Pound Pure white, dry picked 50 " " Stained and scalded white 40 " " Dark or mixed, dry picked 33 " " Dark or mixed, scalded 20 to 25 " "

Marketing Eggs. On commercial duck farms very few eggs are marketed. This is due to the fact that the duck growers find it more profitable to incubate all eggs suitable for that purpose and to rear and market the ducklings rather than to sell the eggs. There are always, however, a certain number of cracked eggs and others which may be too large or too small to use for hatching and which are therefore marketed. In addition the infertile eggs tested out on the 5th day are sold. The eggs may be packed in ordinary 30 dozen egg cases such as are used for hens' eggs, utilizing a special filler 5 cells square. With these fillers a case holds 20 5-6 dozen duck eggs. A special duck case, holding 30 dozen duck eggs may be used, the fillers in this case being 6 cells square like the fillers used for hens' eggs. The cells in these fillers are 2 inches square and 2?or 2?inches deep.

CHAPTER VIII

Duck Raising on the Farm

Duck raising as ordinarily conducted on the general farm consists of the keeping of a comparatively small flock purely as a side line. Ducks on the general farm may be kept for the production of meat and eggs, for egg production, or mainly as a breeding proposition where the idea is to produce birds of exhibition quality. On occasional farms ducks of the rarer breeds are kept mainly for ornamental purposes.

Conditions Suitable for Duck Raising. A small flock of ducks on the farm can be kept to best advantage where they can be separated from the other poultry and where they can have access to a pasture or an orchard which will provide them with a plentiful supply of green feed. Ducks stand confinement quite well but if they are closely confined it is necessary to provide for them the green feed which they cannot secure for themselves. On many farms the flock of ducks is allowed to range at liberty and under these conditions the cost of maintaining them is much lower since they pick up a considerable part of their feed. An enclosed run or yard, however, should be available where they can be confined when desired. It is also necessary to provide a house or shed in which they can be shut at night and during the early morning. Otherwise, many of the eggs may be dropped anywhere about the place or in the water with the result that some of them will be lost. A pond or stream to which the ducks can have access and in which they can swim is a great advantage since it helps to keep them in good breeding condition. It is a common but mistaken idea that low, wet land is best suited for ducks.

Size of Flock.--The average farm flock of ducks is small, rarely running over 15 to 20 head. In many cases not over 10 or 12 ducks with one or two drakes will be kept. A flock of this size will furnish quite a large number of ducks for the farmer's table or for sale in addition to more or less eggs which can either be used at home or sold.

Making a Start. In making a start with a farm flock of ducks it is probably best to figure on keeping only a few head. If the farmer begins with 4 or 5 ducks and one drake he can make his start at small expense and from this number he will be able to increase the size of his flock if he finds that results warrant it. Probably the best way to make a start is to purchase the desired breeding stock in the fall. This will give the ducks a chance to get settled and to be in good condition and accustomed to their quarters by spring so that they will begin to breed and lay.

Eggs for hatching can be purchased if desired and the young ducklings hatched and reared with chicken hens. Baby ducks are rarely purchased in making a start as are baby chicks.

Selecting the Breed. Any one of the breeds forming the so-called meat class will prove satisfactory for a farm flock. This class includes the Pekin, Aylesbury, Muscovy, Rouen, Cayuga, Buff and Blue Swedish. The birds of any of these breeds are of good size and therefore produce a suitable table fowl. At the same time they are layers and will produce eggs for the table or for market as well. Where the purpose in keeping the ducks is mainly that of producing eggs for market the Runner is undoubtedly the breed to select. While these ducks are smaller in size the ducklings will make good carcasses of broiler size for the table being killed for this purpose when about 2?to 3 pounds in weight. In addition, the Runner is the best laying breed and by many persons is considered to be equal in its egg producing qualities to any of the breeds of chickens.

Selection of any breed or variety of the meat or egg classes and especially the selection of a breed or variety for ornamental purposes or for the pleasure of breeding will depend upon the individual preference of the owner for body shape, color of plumage and other characteristics. A pure breed of some kind should by all means be kept in preference to the common or so-called "puddle" duck. Not only will the pure breeds give greater uniformity in the carcasses produced but the results in egg production will likewise be better.

Age of Breeding Stock. The best results in breeding are secured from ducks during their first laying season. Not only is egg production better but they are less likely to become so fat and large as to interfere with the fertility and hatchability of the eggs. In fact, on commercial duck farms the breeding stock is entirely renewed each year. However, ducks can be profitably kept until they are 2 or 3 years old, and it is common practice in a farm flock to hold over some of the breeders after they have finished their first year. Of course, where the duck breeder has some especially fine stock which will produce just the quality he desires in the offspring, he holds and utilizes these birds just as long as they are in good breeding condition. As a rule it is best not to hold breeding ducks after they have finished their second laying season.

Size of Matings. The proper number of ducks which should be mated to a drake varies with the different breeds. Pekins and Aylesbury can be mated in the proportion of one drake to 6 to 8 ducks. In the Rouen mate 4 or 5 ducks to a drake and in the Cayuga 5 or 6 ducks to a drake. In the Muscovy as high as 10 females may be mated with one male. In the Blue Swedish and Buff mate in the proportion of 6 or 7 ducks to one drake. In the Call and East India breeds from 5 to 8 ducks can be mated to one drake. In the Crested White use 5 or 6 ducks and in the Runner 6 to 8 ducks to a drake.

Where young drakes are used more ducks can be mated to them than is the case with old drakes. It is also true that where especially large exhibition birds have been reserved for breeding purposes it is necessary to reduce the number of ducks mated to a drake as otherwise the fertility is very likely to run lower with these older heavier ducks.

Breeding and Laying Season. Under ordinary farm conditions where the ducks receive only fairly good care and feed the laying does not begin to any extent until February or March. With exceptional care the ducks will begin to lay in January and a few may even lay in December. The ducks lay very persistently and continue their laying until hot weather sets in or usually about the first of July. They gradually let up in their laying until it ceases almost entirely soon after that date. The breeding season is at its height in the months of April and May. At this time the fertility will run best and the results in hatching will be most satisfactory. However, it is possible to continue to hatch the duck eggs which are produced with fair results as long as the ducks continue to lay.

Management of Breeders.

Housing. Some sort of house or shelter must be provided for the breeding flock. Any available shed or a part of the poultry house may be utilized for this purpose. No special requirements are necessary except that the house should provide sufficient ventilation. This is best furnished by means of a window and in addition, an opening in the front of the house should be provided which can be closed by means of a curtain during severe winter weather. A board floor is not necessary if the dirt floor is filled up 6 or 8 inches above the ground level outside the house. The floors should be provided with an abundance of litter which is usually changed only once or twice during the year. As the litter tends to become dirty more litter must be added. No equipment is necessary in the houses as the birds rest on the floor and lay their eggs anywhere about the house or wherever they may make their nests. The house should be so arranged that the ducks can be shut in at night and can be kept there until they have finished laying in the morning. As most of the duck eggs are laid early in the morning they can be let out by 8 or 9 o'clock in the summer. If let out earlier than this they are likely to lay some of their eggs in the pond or stream to which they have access and these would be lost.

Feeding. On many farms the breeding flock of ducks is fed on the same ration which is given the farm fowls. However, better results will be obtained if they are given special feeds. After the laying season is over the breeding ducks can be fed sparingly on a mash consisting of one part by weight corn meal, 2 parts bran, 1 part low grade wheat flour, 1 part green feed, 8% beef scrap and 3% oyster shell. This mash is mixed up with water until it has a consistency just between sticky and crumbly. It should never be fed in a sloppy condition. A feed of this mash should be given in the morning and at night and during the long days of summer it is well also to give a light feed of cracked corn or mixed grains in the middle of the day. However, judgment must be used in feeding ducks especially if they have range over which they can roam where they can pick up more or less animal feed and other material. In this case it is not necessary to feed nearly so much. Another mash which may be used instead of the one given consists of 3 parts by measure of corn meal, 4 parts bran, 2 parts low grade wheat flour, three-fourths part beef scrap and 2 parts green feed with a supply of oyster shell.

Along about December 1 the feed should be changed with the idea of inducing egg production. A feed consisting of one part by weight corn meal, 1 part low grade flour or middlings, 1 part bran, 15% beef scrap, 15% vegetables or green feed together with oyster shell should be fed morning and evening and in addition a feed consisting of corn and wheat may be given at noon in a quantity of about one quart for each 30 ducks. As much mash should be given them at the morning and evening feed as they will clean up.

Another good mash feed which may be used consists of 2 parts by weight of bran, 2 parts middlings, 2 parts corn meal, 1 part beef scrap, 1 part ground oats and one-tenth of the total weight sand. In addition, of course, green feed must be added to the ration if it is not available at all times in the yard. This mash is fed in the morning and in the evening. The noon feed consists of 1 part by weight of corn and 2 parts oats. Where green feed is not available and must be supplied, cut clover, alfalfa, rye, oats and corn may be utilized cut up into short pieces and mixed in the mash. The mash should be fed either to breeding stock or to ducklings on flat trays or boards rather than in troughs as the ducks can get at it better in this form. It must be kept in mind that while ducks are good egg producers during the laying and breeding season they will not lay any great number of eggs unless they are fed for this purpose. For rations used on commercial duck farms see Chapter IV.

Water. It is important that a plentiful supply of drinking water be available to the ducks. A fresh supply must be provided at each feeding time before the feed is thrown to the ducks as they like to eat and drink alternately when feeding. Where the breeding ducks have access to a stream or pond of fresh water it is not necessary to provide any other supply of drinking water.

Where water is available in which the ducks can swim it is essential to see that provision is made so that the ducks can get in and out of the water easily. If this is not done they may become exhausted and unable to climb out or they may become partially cramped when the water is very cold with the result that they will drown. If given access to water in which they can swim during cold weather it is necessary to be on the look-out to see that the ducks do not freeze fast to the ground when they come out of the water.

Yards. Where yards are provided for ducks poultry netting about 2 feet high is ordinarily used. This will confine most of the breeds but higher fences even 5 or 6 feet high must be provided for the breeds which fly readily such as the Muscovy, Call, East India, Mallard, Wood and Mandarin. In some cases it is even necessary to cover over the tops of the yards in order to keep the birds from flying out or to pinion the birds, that is, to cut off the outermost joint of one wing. The netting used for yards should be strung on posts set in the ground and the lower edge should be pegged down so that the birds cannot get under it.

Care of Eggs for Hatching. Duck eggs for hatching must be gathered each day and should be put in some cool place to be held until they are set. They should be turned daily, the same as hens' eggs and the general care is exactly similar. It does not, however, pay to keep duck eggs as long before setting them as they spoil more quickly than hens' eggs. In fact, it is best to set duck eggs when they are not over a week old if this can be arranged.

Hatching the Eggs. The period of incubation for duck eggs ranges from 26 to 28 days for all of the breeds except the Muscovy. In this breed it takes from 33 to 36 days for the eggs to hatch. Inasmuch as most of the commonly kept breeds are not very broody and therefore do not make reliable hatchers and mothers it is necessary to resort either to the use of chicken hens for this purpose or else to utilize incubators. Either one of these methods can be used with good success. With the small farm flock it is very common to utilize hens. The ordinary hen will be able to cover 9 to 11 duck eggs to advantage depending on her size and upon the season of the year. In cold weather the smaller number should be used rather than the larger number. Before setting the hen she should be thoroughly dusted with insect powder to free her from lice. Several hens can be set in the same room but they should be confined on their nests allowing them to come off only once a day for feed and water. Cracked corn makes an excellent feed for sitting hens. If desired Muscovy, Call, East India, Mallard, Wood or Mandarin ducks can be allowed to make their nests and to hatch their eggs as they are reliable sitters and good mothers.

After the duck eggs first pip there usually elapses a longer period of time before the ducklings get out of the shell than is the case with chicks. For this reason it is well to take the hens off for feed and water when the first eggs are pipped returning them to the nest as quickly as possible and confining them there until the hatch is over.

During the last week of incubation it is desirable to sprinkle the eggs daily with water using quite a liberal amount as duck eggs seem to require more moisture than hens' eggs in order to hatch well.

All duck eggs which are at all badly soiled should be washed before they are set. Washing does not seem to injure their hatching qualities. In fact, some breeders prefer to wash all duck eggs whether dirty or not, feeling that this opens up the pores and causes a better hatch. This belief is based upon the idea that when ducks hatch their own eggs under natural conditions they have access to water in which they swim and in coming back on the nest their wet feathers serve to wash the eggs.

Where an incubator is used for hatching the eggs are placed in the machine just as hens' eggs. For the first week the temperature is kept about 102 degrees and for the rest of the period is maintained as close to 103 degrees as possible, the bulb of the thermometer being on a level with the tops of the eggs. Often the temperature will run up a little higher than this at hatching time but this does not do any harm. An incubator will accommodate from four-fifths to five-sixths as many duck eggs as it will hens' eggs.

About the fifth or sixth day the duck eggs are tested and all infertile and dead germs removed. From this time on eggs are turned twice a day and usually cooled once a day until they pip. A second test may be made about the fifteenth or sixteenth day when any eggs which have died are removed. If dead germ eggs are left in the machines they spoil very quickly and cause a strong odor which makes it necessary to remove them. During the last week or ten days and in some cases for a longer period than this incubator operators supply moisture daily to the machine. This is usually provided by sprinkling the eggs liberally with water which has been warmed to about the temperature of the machine. However, if warm water is not available, water of ordinary temperature may be used although it is not well to use extremely cold water. As a rule the eggs begin to pip about the twenty-sixth day. At this time the machine should be tightly closed up and left so until the hatching is over. In case moisture seems to be lacking and the ducklings are having a hard time to get out of the shell the machine can be opened and the eggs sprinkled again. If there seems to be sufficient moisture, however, the machines should not be opened or disturbed. As a rule it takes ducklings from 24 to 48 hours to hatch after the pipping first begins. It is advisable to leave the ducklings in the incubator until they are well dried off before removing them to the brooder. As a rule the hatching will be entirely over by the twenty-eighth day.

Brooding and Rearing. Ducklings can be brooded if desired by means of chicken hens. In this case the ducklings which the hen hatches should be given to her and she should be confined to some kind of a coop which will allow the ducklings to run at liberty. If the hen is given her liberty she goes too far and takes too much exercise for the little ducks. Where artificial brooders are used any type of brooding apparatus can be utilized which is used with success for chickens. It must be remembered, however, that ducklings do not require as high a degree of heat as do baby chicks and should be started off at a temperature of about 90 degrees under the hover. This can be reduced rather rapidly until it is down to 80 at about 2 weeks of age. The length of time that the ducklings require heat after this depends upon the season and the weather. Even in fairly cool weather they do not need any heat after they are 5 or 6 weeks old.

It is necessary to keep the brooders clean and in order to do this they must be cleaned out frequently and new litter supplied. While the ducklings are small the brooders should be cleaned at least every other day and as they get larger, cleaning once a week with the addition of fresh litter between times will be sufficient.

Feeding the Ducklings. Ducklings do not need to be fed until they are from 24 to 36 hours old. At this time they may be given a mixture composed of equal parts by measure of rolled oats and bread crumbs with 3% of sharp sand mixed in the feed. This may be given them five times daily although some duck raisers feed only 3 times daily from the start. About the third day this feed is changed to equal parts of bread, rolled oats, bran and corn meal. After the seventh day the ration may consist of 3 parts bran, 1 part each of low-grade wheat flour and corn meal, 10% green feed, 5% beef scrap with about 3% of sand mixed in.

The ducklings should be fed four times daily after the seventh day until they are two or three weeks old. After that time they need be fed only three times daily, morning, noon and night. The sand may be given to the ducklings either by mixing it in the mash or by feeding it in a hopper where they can help themselves. The mash feed which is prepared for the ducklings is mixed with water until it has a consistency a little wetter than crumbly but not exactly sticky. Sloppy feed should never be used. As the ducklings grow older the amount of beef scrap can be increased until it consists of 15% of the ration by the end of the third week. The proportion of corn meal can likewise be increased and simultaneously the amount of bran decreased until the ducklings are on a fattening ration. Unless they have a plentiful supply of green feed in the yards to which they have access it is necessary to provide this to the extent of about 10% of the feed and it should consist of tender green stuff rather finely chopped and mixed in with the mash.

About 2 weeks before the ducklings are to be marketed they should be put on a ration consisting of three parts by weight of corn meal, two parts low-grade flour or middlings, one part bran, one-half part beef scrap, 10% green feed and about 3% oyster shell or sand. This mash is fed three times daily. Another ration which can be used for fattening purposes consists of 3 parts corn meal, 1 part low-grade wheat flour, 1 part bran, 5% beef scrap and 3% oyster shell with green feed and grit in addition.

Where fish is available it can be substituted for the beef scrap but on most farms this is impractical. The fish where fed is boiled and mixed in the mash. However, no fish should be fed up to within 2 weeks before the ducks are killed as there is danger of giving a fishy taste to the carcass. For additional information as to feeding methods used on commercial duck farms which could be utilized to advantage for the farm flocks, see Chapter VI.

Birds which are to be reserved for breeders should be selected out and taken away from the ducklings which are to be fattened. These breeding birds should be carried along on the ration which they have been receiving until about December 1 when they should be put on a laying ration.

It is very necessary to see that the ducklings have a plentiful supply of drinking water. It is especially important to renew this supply just before the ducklings are fed so that they will have ample water while they are consuming their feed. The water should be given in dishes deep enough so that the ducks can immerse their entire bill as this enables them to wash the sand out of their nostrils.

Water for Ducklings. In addition to the drinking water provided duck raisers sometimes allow the growing ducklings access to water in which they can swim. If it is desired to fatten the ducklings quickly and turn them off on the market as green ducks many raisers do not consider this advisable as it induces the ducklings to take more exercise and makes it more difficult to fatten them. However, access to water in which they can swim makes it unnecessary to provide any other supply of drinking water and for this reason lessens the work considerably. Unless it is easy for the ducklings to get in and out of the water there is danger of some of them drowning as they are likely to get tired and unable to climb out. Little ducklings allowed access to very cold water are subject to cramp and may be drowned as a result.

Distinguishing the Sexes. It is difficult to distinguish the sexes of growing ducks until they begin to reach maturity. There is, however, a difference in their appearance. The drakes are coarser or thicker and more masculine in appearance showing this especially about the head and neck. Also as they secure their mature plumage the drake shows curled feathers on top of the tail which are often referred to as sex feathers. In addition, the voice of the duck is harsher and coarser than that of the drake.

Marketing the Ducks. Most of the ducks produced on farms are marketed alive. This is because the farmer has no special market and he does not find that it pays him to dress and ship the ducks with the chance that they might spoil. In fact, most of the farm raised ducks are not turned off as green ducks at 10 to 12 weeks as is done on the commercial duck plants but are held until fall and then sold as spring ducks. They will weigh somewhat more at that time but as a rule the price received per pound will be lower than that obtained for green ducks during the spring and summer. Where there is a special demand for ducklings which the farmer can supply it will pay him to dress and deliver the ducks. If it is desired to dress the ducks, the directions given under Chapter VII can be modified to suit the farmer's needs. The soft body feathers should be saved in accordance with the directions given on page 106, as they can be used at home in making pillows or can be sold.

Such eggs as are produced in surplus may either be utilized on the home table or sent to market. As a rule duck eggs are not in great demand except at certain seasons such as at Easter and during the Jewish holidays in the spring and fall when they bring somewhat higher prices than hens' eggs. The larger size of duck eggs, however, makes them favored by bakers and they can usually be sold at any time in a city of any size at prices as good as those received for hens' eggs.

Eggs for market can be packed in the ordinary 30-dozen hen egg cases by using special fillers which hold 25 eggs instead of 36 as in the case of hens' eggs. See page 119. A farmer with a small flock of ducks will usually not have eggs enough to fill a case frequently and for this reason he usually finds it more convenient to market the few eggs he has by taking them into town in a basket.

Disease and Insect Pests. Ducks are very little troubled by insect pests, nor are they greatly troubled by diseases. The usual difficulties encountered along this line are those discussed under this head in

Chapter VI.

Losses are often experienced as the result of predatory animals. Rats will cause a great amount of havoc among the young ducks if they are able to get at them. A single night's work on the part of one rat may practically clean out a small flock of ducklings. It is necessary to make sure that the ducklings are shut in at night so that rats cannot get at them.

GEESE

PART II.

CHAPTER IX

Extent of the Industry--Opportunities

Geese can be raised successfully in practically all parts of the United States and are in fact scattered in small flocks over a considerable portion of the country being most abundant in the South and in the Middle West.

The census figures for the year 1920 show Illinois with 195,769 geese to be the leading state in numbers, closely followed by Missouri, Arkansas and Iowa. Next in order of importance as goose raising states come Kentucky, Tennessee, Minnesota, North Carolina and Texas. The census figures of 1920 compared with those for 1910 show a decrease in the number of geese from 4,431,980 to 2,939,203. The only groups of states which showed an increase in the number of geese during this period were the North Atlantic and the Mountain states. Of the total farms in the United States only a small proportion, probably one-tenth, have any geese and the number of geese per farm would not average over 4 to 10 depending on the section.

Nature of the Industry. Geese are kept almost wholly in small flocks as a side line on general farms. The purpose of goose raising is primarily one of the production of meat although in the past flocks of geese have been kept to some extent, particularly in the south for the purpose of plucking them to secure the feathers. This practice of plucking live geese is decreasing and is much less common than formerly. The eggs of the geese do not enter to any extent into the egg trade of the country. As a rule all the eggs produced are hatched for the purpose of rearing young geese and it is only occasionally that goose eggs are used for culinary purposes.

Opportunities for Goose Raising. Undoubtedly the greatest opportunity along the line of goose raising lies in the small flock kept on the general farm. Where conditions are suitable, that is to say, where there is an abundance of suitable pasture land together with some water to which the geese can have access, a small flock can be most profitably kept. They can be reared very cheaply as both the young and old geese will secure practically their entire living during the summer from pasture if an abundant supply of suitable green material is available. The cost of rearing them therefore is low. In addition both the young and old geese are very hardy and require comparatively little care. They are little subject to disease and therefore losses are small.

Geese live and breed for a long time and this makes it possible to turn off to market a larger proportion of the young stock reared than is the case with most other classes of poultry. For all of these reasons, therefore, a small flock of geese will return a good profit to the farmer without having to supply any great amount of equipment or without having to feed very much in the way of expensive feeds. In addition to the geese which can be marketed, the maintenance of a small flock also helps to provide a variety in the farmer's diet by furnishing suitable birds for the holiday seasons such as Thanksgiving and Christmas.

In addition to the opportunity for goose raising in small flocks on general farms there likewise exists a definite opportunity to specialize along this line somewhat more extensively. In certain places, notably the state of Wisconsin, goose raising becomes a more important activity on some farms than merely that of a by-product. Larger numbers are reared and special steps are taken in fattening and finishing them for market either by means of pen fattening or by means of hand fattening or noodling the geese. Geese so finished for market bring a special price and allow a good profit to the raiser for the time which he has put into them.

An outgrowth of the goose raising industry which has been worked to a limited extent consists of the gathering together of the geese raised in any particular portion of the country on one farm and the feeding of them there in large flocks in the fields so as to fatten them for market. There are not many of these special fattening farms but several persons in different sections of the country who have made a practice of gathering together and marketing the geese in this way have found it very profitable. Probably a similar opportunity exists in certain other sections where goose raising on the farms in small numbers is common and where no one has yet made the effort to collect and fatten the geese before marketing them.

While geese are not exhibited to the same extent as chickens, still there will always be found a market for birds of good quality, both for the purpose of exhibition and also as breeders to be used in improving the stock of other goose raisers.

Goose Raising as a Business for Farm Women. Like turkey raising goose raising as a side line on the farm offers an excellent money making opportunity for the farm women. Without any great outlay of capital to get a start and without its being necessary to provide much in the way of buildings or other equipment, a flock of geese can be started which will allow a nice profit to the farm woman for the care and attention which she gives them. In this connection it should be remembered that while the opportunities for profit may not be so large as in turkey raising, yet the care required is much less and the chances of serious difficulties due to disease and to inability to raise the young stock are relatively small. Goose raising therefore offers a most profitable side line employment for the farm woman.

Geese as Weed Destroyers. As stated before geese are close grazers. In fact, during the growing season of the year green vegetation forms most and in some cases practically all of their diet. The vegetation which they will eat readily is quite varied and in many cases geese will be found to be very valuable in ridding pastures or fields of troublesome weeds. In the southern states geese are often kept on farms where cotton is raised for the purpose of keeping the cotton fields free from weeds.

Objection to Geese

An objection to geese often expressed but without good foundation is that they will spoil the pasture for other stock. This is not true if the pasture is not overstocked with geese. Of course geese are very close grazers and if too many of them are kept on a field they will eat the grass down so close that there will be none for other animals to get. Similarly the idea that other animals will not eat grass grown where goose droppings have fallen is not true except where the birds are too thick so that the grass is soiled badly by the droppings.

The fact that geese are noisy creatures makes them undesirable to some persons. It is true that they make a good deal of noise and that their cry is of a very hoarse, rasping character and to a person with bad nerves they may be annoying but this is no valid or weighty objection to the normal, healthy farmer. The Chinese geese are the noisiest and consequently the greatest offenders in this particular.

A more valid objection to geese lies in the fact of their rather ugly disposition. Ganders, especially as they grow older and during the breeding season, are decidedly pugnacious and will not hesitate to attack human beings. They strike heavy formidable blows with their wings and with their strong bills they inflict most painful bites. Where there are children about the house it may be necessary to dispose of ugly ganders to safeguard the children from serious injury.

CHAPTER X

Breeds and Varieties--How to Mate to Produce Exhibition Specimens--Preparing Geese for the Show--Catching and Handling

Breeds of Geese. There are six standard breeds of geese consisting of the following: Toulouse, Embden, African, Chinese, Wild or Canadian and Egyptian. All of these breeds consist of a single variety with the exception of the Chinese which is composed of two. The Toulouse is known as the Gray Toulouse, the Embden as the White Embden, the African as the Gray African, the two varieties of the Chinese as the Brown Chinese and the White Chinese, the Wild or Canadian as the Gray and the Egyptian as the Colored.

The first four of these breeds are the ones which are commonly kept in domestication. In a general way it may be said that these breeds are meat breeds for the reason that they are kept mainly for the production of meat. The Wild or Canadian and the Egyptian are more in the nature of ornamental breeds since they are not so commonly kept and are principally to be found where ornamental water-fowls are maintained. The Chinese are sometimes classed as ornamental geese on account of their smaller size but they are much more commonly kept than either the Canadian or the Egyptian and make a good market fowl where the demand is not for such a large carcass.

In addition to the standard breeds there are several other rare breeds among which is the Sebastapol which is kept purely as an ornamental breed by reason of its peculiar feathering. The Sebastapol is a white goose in which the feathers of the upper part of the body show a twisted or frizzled condition which gives it much the general effect of the feathers being curled. In addition to the standard breeds of geese there are kept on a great majority of farms ordinary common geese of no definite breed or variety. These geese in general are of smaller size than the larger standard breeds and have probably arisen as the result of the crossing of the standard breeds and the subsequent deterioration in size and color marking is due to careless breeding and selection.

In some sections and for certain special purposes definite crosses of standard breeds are made for the production of table geese having certain desired qualities. For this purpose the African ganders are very popular used upon the Toulouse geese. To some extent there is produced and marketed a goose known as the mongrel goose. This has excellent table quality and is in good demand on account of its superior eating qualities and its rapid growth. It is produced by using the Wild or Canadian gander upon Toulouse, African or Embden geese. The result of this cross is a hybrid goose which has much the appearance of the Wild goose but which will not breed although the females will lay eggs. As a rule Toulouse or African females are used for the cross rather than Embden as from the latter there is a greater tendency to get a lighter cross which would not resemble its Wild father so closely and might not therefore be so readily recognized as genuine mongrel geese.

Nomenclature. The term geese is used to indicate the birds of both sexes taken as a whole and also as a plural form for the word goose. The term goose is used to distinguish the female of the species. The male is given the specific name of gander to distinguish it from goose. The young of both sexes are termed goslings. In giving the standard weights for the different breeds of geese the birds are classified as adult ganders and young ganders and as adult geese and young geese. By adult goose or gander is meant a bird which is over one year old, by young goose or gander is meant a bird which is less than one year. Not infrequently in connection with market reports use will be made of the term "green geese". This indicates birds which are marketed when they are of large size but still young and immature, the green referring to this immature condition.

Size. An idea of the size of the different standard breeds of geese can best be secured by giving the standard weights. They are as follows:

Breed Adult Adult Young Young Gander Goose Gander Goose

Toulouse 26 lbs. 20 lbs. 20 lbs. 16 lbs. Embden 20 " 18 " 18 " 16 " African 20 " 18 " 16 " 14 " Chinese 12 " 10 " 10 " 8 " Wild or Canadian 12 " 10 " 10 " 8 " Egyptian 10 " 8 " 8 " 6 "

Popularity of the Breeds. Of the different standard breeds kept the Toulouse is undoubtedly the most popular in this country probably due to its large size as well as to its quick growth. The Embden follows the Toulouse closely in popularity. The Chinese geese are probably third most numerous in numbers while the African ranks fourth. In certain sections the African seems to be very popular and one would expect to find more of this breed than seem to be present on farms. Neither the Canadian nor the Egyptians are to be found in any great numbers, the latter in particular being very rare.

Egg Production

It must always be remembered in speaking of the egg production of any breed of poultry that there will be a considerable variation in individuals within a breed and that egg production will also be affected very largely by the conditions under which the birds are kept. For this reason any attempt to give an average egg production for a breed is at best only an approximation. These approximations often serve, however, to show some well established contrast between the different breeds with respect to their egg laying ability. The Toulouse is a fairly prolific breed of geese and individuals should average from 12 to 36 eggs, the majority laying about 20 eggs. The Embden is very similar to the Toulouse in laying ability although probably on the whole not quite so good a layer. The African is generally considered a good layer and is said to average from 20 to 40 eggs. Some breeders state that the pure African are not as good layers as this, being about equal to the Embden and that the better laying Africans really have some Brown Chinese blood in them which has been introduced to increase prolificacy. The Chinese is the most prolific breed. The birds of either the White or Brown variety should average from 60 to 100 eggs. The eggs laid by the Chinese are smaller than those of the Toulouse, Embden or African. The Wild or Canadian and the Egyptian geese are small layers. They rarely lay more than one sitting during a season and the eggs will as a rule range from 4 to 8 in number.

Size of Goose Eggs. Goose eggs are decidedly larger than duck eggs. There is a considerable variation in size, depending upon the breed. The eggs of the Toulouse, African and Embden are of about the same size and will vary from 6?to 8 ounces each. The eggs of the Chinese are smaller and will weigh from 5?to 6 ounces each, while eggs of the Canadian and Egyptian are the smallest of the standard breeds, running from 5 to 5?ounces each.

Color of Goose Eggs. In general goose eggs are whitish in color but may shade to a gray or buff tinge. The Wild or Canadian sometimes lay eggs which are off the white, showing a considerable green tinge.

About Geese and Matings

Broodiness. All of the breeds of geese with the exception of the Toulouse may be classed as broody breeds, that is to say, they will make their nests and hatch their young if given a chance to do so. Not infrequently individuals of the Toulouse breed will do this also but as a rule they are not dependable for this purpose.

Size of Mating. In making the mating it is usual in order to secure best results to use one gander with from two to four geese in the Toulouse, Embden and African breeds. In fact, better results will be secured in these breeds where not over 3 geese are used and in many cases the geese are mated in trios or even in pairs. In the Chinese geese a somewhat larger mating can be employed, one gander being used with 4 to 6 geese. The Wild or Canadian and the Egyptian geese in most cases pair only.

Age of Breeders. Geese can be retained and will give good results as breeders for a longer period than most other classes of poultry. While the young geese will often lay during their first year the results from the eggs produced by them are not as a rule very satisfactory. It is sometimes claimed that the eggs of young geese will not hatch but this is untrue and goslings have been raised from such eggs. Canadian and Egyptian geese do not lay until they are 3 years old. Females may be kept for breeding purposes until they are 8 to 10 years old and should give good results during this time. If they continue to lay longer than this and are valuable breeding individuals they should of course be retained just so long as they lay at a profitable rate. Instances are reported where geese 15 to 20 years old were still giving good results as breeders. As a rule ganders cannot be successfully kept for breeding purposes as long as can the geese. Yearling ganders are often used but they are at their best for breeding purposes when from 3 to 5 years old and it is not generally wise to retain them after they are 6 or 7 years old. Egyptian and Canadian ganders will not breed before they are 2 years old. In general it is good practice to mate young ganders to older geese and to mate younger geese with older ganders as this seems to get better results both in fertility and in hatching.

Marking Young Geese. It is often desirable to mark young geese in some way so that their breeding can be told or so that a record can be kept of their age. This can be readily accomplished by punching various combinations of holes in the webs between the toes at the time the goslings are hatched.

Considerations in Making the Mating.[4] In making the mating in breeding geese it must be kept in mind that it is of primary importance to select the breeders first of all for size, prolificacy and vitality. Without these qualities no matter what else the breeding geese may be there is scant chance of satisfactory results. Having selected birds which are of suitable size and vitality those should then be utilized for breeding which approach most nearly both in type and color to the requirements as given in the American Standard of Perfection. As a rule, a new mating can be made by taking the birds selected and shutting them up together in a pen away from the other birds and out of sound of the voices of their former mates. As a rule about a month of this treatment will suffice to bring about the new matings desired and the birds can then be allowed to range at liberty.

[Footnote 4: For a more detailed description of the principles of breeding as applied to poultry and which is equally applicable to geese, the reader is referred to "The Mating and Breeding of Poultry" by Harry M. Lamon and Rob R. Slocum, published by the Orange Judd Publishing Co., New York, N. Y.]

Some ganders are very troublesome about mating. This is particularly true as they get older. In some cases it is impossible to get ganders to mate at all while frequently they will refuse to mate with more than one goose. As a rule, matings once made are permanent from year to year unless changed by the breeder on account of poor results. Where new matings are to be made or where changes are to be made this should be done in the fall so that the birds will have been mated for several months before the breeding season begins in order to insure good results. After the matings are made the geese can be allowed to run together in larger flocks but the practice is frequently employed of keeping the different matings in pens to themselves so as to avoid the fighting which will otherwise occur between the ganders. During the breeding season the ganders are quite savage and will fight fiercely.

Breeds of Geese[5]

The Toulouse. This breed is characterized by its very low down deep broad massive body. The body should come well down in front and should be so deep and full behind that it tends to drag on the ground when the bird walks. The skin of the rear portion of the body should have folds. The appearance or type of the Toulouse depends a great deal upon the condition of flesh which a bird may be in at the time as a fat well fleshed condition will improve type very materially. A dewlap, that is to say, a pendulous flap of skin on the throat, is desired but comparatively few birds show a well developed dewlap. It is more likely to appear with age than it is in the younger birds. In color the Toulouse breeds quite true. The principal difficulty which is encountered is the occasional appearance of one, two or three white flight feathers in the wing. These white flights constitute a disqualification and must of course be avoided in the breeding. It is necessary also to avoid any birds which lack in size, length, breadth or depth of body, particularly depth in front. Birds of this breed are of large size and make quick growth and for this reason are a fine market goose although the dark colored pin feathers are somewhat of a drawback from a market point of view.

[Footnote 5: For a complete and official description and list of disqualifications of the standard breeds and varieties of geese, the reader is referred to the American Standard of Perfection published by the American Poultry Association, obtainable from Orange Judd Publishing Company, New York, N. Y.]

The Embden. This breed is of good size but somewhat smaller than the Toulouse. It has not quite so long a keel or underline as the Toulouse and while deep in body it is not so baggy. There should be no dewlap in this breed. The plumage should be pure white throughout, the only difficulty of any importance occurring here being the occasional appearance of slate on the backs of young geese. This, however, is not serious as it almost invariably disappears with the first moult. Embden geese are rapid growers and mature early which together with the fact that their plumage is white makes them an excellent market bird.

The African. In type the African is much the same as the Toulouse although not quite as large being about the size of the Embden. What is desired is a low down body which is flat in keel and without any folds of skin. The neck should be short. This bird unlike the Toulouse is characterized by a knob or protuberance extending out from the head at the base of the upper bill. This knob should be black in color and should show no tinge of yellow on the top or about the base. If the knob gets scarred or injured it is apt to turn yellow and freezing likewise is apt to cause it to turn yellow. Birds of this breed both young and old should show dewlaps, the absence of these in adult specimens constituting a disqualification. As in the Toulouse avoid any white flight feathers. The African makes an excellent market goose being like the Embden and Toulouse, quick growing and early maturing. The ganders are especially in favor for use in crossing with other varieties for the production of market geese. It seems probable that some Brown Chinese blood has been crossed into the Africans on various occasions probably for the purpose of increasing the prolificacy of the African as the Brown Chinese is an excellent layer. It is also true that crosses between the Brown Chinese and the Toulouse are sometimes shown for Africans but as a rule this cross results in too dark a bird and such crosses should never be used for breeding purposes since they would not continue to give the uniformity and other qualities obtained in the first generation.

The Chinese. The Chinese is quite different in type from the three preceding breeds. It is much smaller and higher set on legs and has a body much more upright in carriage. The neck is long and slender and the head has a large knob. An important part about the type is to secure a very slender neck, another important point being to secure a very large knob; the larger this is the better. There is, however, a decided tendency for the knob to run small when the neck is slender and it is difficult to secure in perfection the combination of a very slender neck and a large knob. The Chinese geese should be in good condition but should not be too fat when shown as too good a condition of flesh injures the type materially. If fat there is a decided tendency for the birds to bag down behind which is undesirable. The Chinese geese are the best layers but the egg which they lay is smaller. On account of their smaller size they do not make as good market geese where large sized carcasses are desired but where smaller carcasses suitable for family use are in demand the Chinese make a satisfactory market breed.

The Brown Chinese. In this variety the knob should be dark brown or black. As in the African, injury or freezing may turn the knob yellow which is undesirable. The plumage should be a rich brown shade of color, a faded gray color being very undesirable. The stripe down the back of the neck should be well defined and should be distinctly in contrast with the rest of the neck color. White feathers in the primaries or secondaries must be avoided.

The White Chinese. The knob in this variety should be orange and any tendency toward yellow should be avoided. The plumage should be pure white throughout. Occasional young females may show slate in the back but this is not serious as it almost invariably disappears with the first moult.

The Wild or Canadian. Contrary to expectation this breed when domesticated is very peaceable and very tame. There is often, however, a tendency for them to grow uneasy when the migratory season comes. To keep the birds from flying away it is necessary to clip the flight feathers of one wing or what is safer still to pinion the bird. Pinioning consists of cutting off the first joint of one wing. This may be done when the birds are small or may be done at any time and does not seem to bother them much. One of the best ways to accomplish this is to break the joint and then cut it off by using a chisel and hammer. Not much bleeding will result but it is well to put a little iodine on the cut. These birds breed very true in type and color and progress in the mating simply consists of continuing to select those birds for breeders which show markings in the greatest excellence. In type a Canadian goose is quite different from that of the other breeds mentioned. It is smaller, set much higher on legs and its body is neater and trimmer, and is oblong and carried in a horizontal position. The neck is long and slender. These birds mate only in pairs as a rule and the females do not mature and lay until they are three years old. The ganders often breed when they are two years old. Usually only a single sitting of eggs is laid consisting of from 4 to 8. Usually, however, all of these eggs will hatch and the young prove to be strong and easily reared.

The Egyptian. This is the smallest of the standard breeds of geese. In type it more nearly approaches the Canadian than any other breed but it is somewhat longer in legs, showing more of the thigh beneath the body. The body is not carried in quite such a horizontal position as the Canadian but slopes downward slightly from the breast to the tail. The neck is neither so long nor quite so slender as that of the Canadian. This breed is the brightest colored of any of the geese and breeds fairly true in color and markings. Like the Canadian the Egyptian goose is likely to become uneasy at times and one wing should therefore be pinioned or the flight feathers clipped to keep the birds from flying away. Like the Canadian the Egyptians mate in pairs only and lay but one sitting during the year. The females do not lay until they are three years old.

Neither the Egyptian nor the Canadian geese should be closely confined or no eggs will be laid. The goose should be allowed to make her own nest and hatch her eggs.

Preparing Geese for the Show

The preparation of geese for the show is comparatively a simple matter. It requires first of all that individuals shall be selected which approach nearest to the standard requirements both in type and in color. As to the actual preparation for exhibition the geese are practically self-prepared. For a period of at least a week or ten days before they are shipped to the show they should be given access to a grass range and to running water. The grass range tends to put them in good condition while the running water will give them an opportunity to clean themselves. Any broken feathers should be plucked at least six weeks before the birds are to be shown so as to give them an opportunity to grow in new ones.

Since all of the common breeds of geese, with the exception of the Chinese, should be shown in a fat condition in order to give them their best type they should be given a grain mixture twice daily for a period of at least ten days before the show in order to get them in good flesh and to bring them up to standard weight. This ration should consist of one part corn and two parts oats. In Chinese geese where it is desired to have them in good condition of flesh but without showing any tendency toward bagginess, oats alone should be fed as they are apt to put on too much fat when corn is fed as well. When the birds are shipped to the show they are quite likely to get their plumage soiled during the journey. If this occurs fill a barrel about half full of water. As the geese are taken from the shipping coops place two of them at a time in the barrel, cover it over and leave them for a few minutes. Then take them out and they will usually be clean.

Catching and Handling Geese

Never catch geese by the legs which are weak and are easily broken or injured. For the same reason they should never be carried by the legs. In catching geese grasp them by the neck just below the head. Often a crooked stick is of value in getting hold of the birds by the neck. Geese can be carried short distances by the neck without injury but it is not advisable to carry them for any considerable distance in this manner, particularly if they are fat. The best way to handle the geese is to catch them by the neck, then place one arm over the shoulders and around the bird's body thus holding the wings in place while both legs are grasped with the hand. The neck should be held with the other hand to keep the bird from biting. In releasing the bird in a pen or shipping coop do not let go of the neck until the bird is placed where it is wanted.

[Illustration: FIG. 54--Proper manner of picking up and carrying geese with the head and neck under the arm. (Photographs from the Bureau of Animal Industry, U. S. Department of Agriculture.)]

Packing and Shipping Hatching Eggs

Goose eggs for hatching must be shipped when they are fresh if they are to be received in good condition and are to give good results in hatching. They can be shipped long distances either by express or by parcel post. In order to prevent breakage and to lessen the effects of the jar to which the eggs are subjected during shipment they should be carefully packed in a market basket or other suitable receptacle. The same method of packing the eggs should be employed as with duck eggs described on page 137.

Prices for Breeding Stock

While the demand for breeding stock is not so broad with geese as it is with some other classes of poultry, there does exist a steady and profitable demand for this class of fowls. Goose eggs for hatching are usually sold in sittings of 5 and the price varies somewhat depending upon the variety. As a rule, Embden and Toulouse eggs will bring from 60 cents to $1.20 each. Chinese goose eggs will bring from 40 cents to $1 each while the eggs of the African goose will bring from $1 to $2 each. Of course the price of eggs for hatching like that of breeding birds depends on the quality of the stock. The prices for the birds themselves for breeding purposes will run anywhere from about $8 to $10 apiece for good birds suitable for breeding on farm flocks, to $25 or even $50 each of birds of especially fine quality.

CHAPTER XI

Management of Breeding Geese

Range for Breeders. Since grass or other vegetation, when plentiful, will furnish practically the entire living both for breeding and growing geese, it is by all means desirable to have suitable range for the breeding stock. Aside from economy of production range is desirable from the fact that the breeders keep in better condition and better results in breeding and fertility are obtained. The range for breeding geese should therefore consist of grass land or pasture. Often rather low wet land can be used for this purpose, particularly if some higher land is also available to provide a more favorable kind of grass. Often geese can be ranged on the same pasture with horses or cattle. Later in the season after the harvest, both breeding and growing geese can be given the range of the stubble fields to good advantage as they will glean most of the shelled grain. The entire flock of breeders is generally allowed to run together but the flock may be divided if desired, or each mating may be kept in a colony by itself if the fighting of the ganders proves troublesome.

Number of Geese to the Acre. The number of geese which can be kept or run to the acre depends of course upon the nature of the land available for the purpose. The better the pasture and therefore the more green feed available throughout the summer and fall, the more geese can be run. In general, the practice is to run from 4 to 25 geese to an acre; ten is a fair average under normal conditions.

Water for Breeding Geese. While water to which the geese can have access for swimming is not absolutely essential for their well being, they like it and it is well to provide water if possible especially during the breeding season. It not only takes care of the problem of supplying drinking water, but in the opinion of many goose raisers, increases the fertility of the eggs laid. A natural water supply such as a stream or pond in the pasture is therefore desirable, but if none is available an artificial pond or tank can be furnished to good advantage.

Distinguishing the Sex. It is difficult to distinguish the sex of geese. It is, of course, necessary to know the sex so as to provide the proper number of ganders and so as to know what birds to pen together in making a mating. Once the sex of a bird is determined it is well for the novice to mark it by means of a suitable leg band so that its sex can be easily distinguished in the future.

It is more difficult to distinguish the sex of young than of old geese. The gander is generally slightly larger and coarser than the goose, with a longer, thicker neck and larger head. The gander also has a shriller cry than the goose whose cry consists of a harsher sound. Some goose raisers claim that they can distinguish the sex of mature geese by the body shape, the underline of the body of the gander from the tail to the point where the legs join the body being nearly straight, while in the goose this line tends to round out with the fuller development of the abdomen. This difference is more marked during the laying season than at other times. Considerable experience is necessary in order to distinguish sex by any of the means described and the really sure way is by an examination of the sexual organs or by observing the actions of the geese when mating.

Upon examination the sphincter muscle which closes the anus of the female when stretched will be found to have a folded appearance. If the gander is placed upon his back and pressure applied around the anus, the penis will protrude. This test is more easily made on a mature than on an immature gander and is also easier to make during warm than during cold weather.

Purchase of Breeding Stock. Geese when mated usually stay mated permanently. Matings are not, therefore, changed from year to year as a rule so long as they continue to give satisfactory results. If it becomes necessary to make new matings or to break up old matings, this should be done in the fall, so that the birds will be thoroughly used to the new order of things by the time the breeding season arrives, and the results in eggs laid and young stock grown will not, therefore, be adversely affected. For this reason, any breeding stock purchased should be secured in the fall rather than to wait until just before the breeding season opens. As a rule, also, a better selection of breeding stock to choose from is available to the purchaser in the fall.

Time of Laying. Geese start laying in the early spring and continue to lay throughout the spring. With special attention given to the feeding, they should begin in the northeastern part of the United States about February 1 and should continue to lay until about June 1 when geese of the heavier breeds such as the Toulouse, African and Embden will generally be pretty well through. Some individuals will lay later than this and the Chinese geese also have a rather longer laying season extending further into the summer. The length of the laying season is also affected by whether the geese are broken up when they become broody or whether they are allowed to sit. The latter practice, of course, stops the layings. It must be remembered that the Canadian and Egyptian as a rule lay only a single small setting of eggs during the season.

As a rule geese lay during the night or the forenoon. The frequency of laying varies, some geese laying every other day while others lay more or less often.

Housing. Geese withstand the weather very well and do not need much in the way of houses or shelter except during winter and during severe storms. In the North it is the usual practice and good practice to provide shelter for the geese, which may take the form of a poultry house, or of any shed or barn available for the purpose. A shed with openings on the south side makes an ideal goose shelter or house. Most breeders in the South who give their flocks good attention also provide shelter for them during the winter although geese are also successfully kept in that section without shelter.

The houses provided for the breeders must be kept clean and as dry as possible. The best way to do this is to bed them liberally with straw, shavings or some similar material, especially during the winter. As the bedding becomes soiled, more should be added and the house should be cleaned out from time to time and fresh litter put in.

No equipment for the houses is necessary. The geese will lay their eggs in nests which they make on the floor and if plenty of clean bedding is provided, the eggs will not get badly soiled. Large boxes, barrels, or similar shelter provided with an abundance of nesting material may be scattered about the range to provide places in which the geese may make their nests.

Yards. Usually no yards are provided for geese as they are allowed the range of a pasture or are allowed to roam at liberty about the farm. Any ordinary woven wire stock fence such as might be used to fence a pasture will serve to keep the geese confined as well as the other stock. If for any reason it is desired to confine geese to a yard, the effort should be made to provide yard enough so that the geese will have a constant supply of green feed. In a small yard this is impossible. A 2?or 3 foot fence is high enough to confine any of the common breeds of geese and will also serve for Canadian and Egyptian geese if they have been pinioned which should always be done.

Feeding the Breeding Geese. While the flock of geese may be allowed to pick most of their living from a good grass range during the summer and fall, it is necessary to feed them during the winter. In fact during the summer it may be necessary to feed them lightly on grain or wet mash if the pasture gets short. The quantity of feed necessary for this purpose depends upon the condition of the pasture and must be judged by the condition of the birds.

During the winter, they must be fed regularly. The feed given them should consist of both grain and some form of roughage. It is necessary to be careful not to overfeed so that the geese will become too fat, for while they should be in good condition of flesh at the beginning of the breeding season, if they are too fat, poor fertility and poor hatches will result.

Feed. Oats makes the best feed for breeding geese as it is not too fattening. Corn, wheat or barley fed alone is likely to prove too fattening but a limited quantity should be fed for variety. The grain should be fed twice a day throughout the winter and should be given rather sparingly, depending on roughage to make up the bulk of the feed. Vegetables, clover or alfalfa hay, chopped corn stover or silage make good roughage for this purpose. Corn silage is a fine feed if it is not moldy and does not contain so much corn as to be too fattening.

About three weeks or a month before it is desired to have the geese commence laying, which should be at such a time that the first goslings hatched will have good grass pasture, a mash should be added to the feed to stimulate egg production. This mash is generally fed in the morning with the vegetables or roughage and may consist of three parts bran or shorts, one part corn meal and one-fourth part meat scrap. If available buttermilk or skim milk can be used to mix the mash and replace the meat scrap. Another mash for this purpose consists of corn meal one-fourth part, bran two parts, and ground oats one part, mixed up with skim milk or buttermilk.

Grit and oyster shell should be kept where the geese can help themselves particularly during the laying season. Drinking water must be available at all times and if a natural supply is not available, must be given in drinking fountains or dishes which should be so arranged that the geese cannot get their feet into the water. When they can get into the drinking water, they will quickly get it into a filthy condition.

When the geese are running in a field with horses or cattle a small enclosure should be fenced in to which the geese can gain access by means of suitable openings but which will keep the other stock out. In this should be placed the drinking fountain for the geese and in this enclosure the geese should be fed. Otherwise the cattle or horses will get most of the feed intended for the geese and in addition, some of the geese may be stepped on or kicked and injured when the stock crowds around at feeding time.

CHAPTER XII

Incubation

Care of Eggs for Hatching. Since egg production usually begins early in the spring while the weather is still cold, it is necessary to gather the eggs at frequent intervals to prevent their freezing or becoming chilled. Later in the season daily collection will be satisfactory. The eggs as collected should be kept in a cool place and where the evaporation of the egg contents will not be too great. If set at fairly frequent intervals, there will be no difficulty on this score. If they are to be kept for some time, they may be stored in bran to prevent evaporation. It is well to mark the eggs as gathered with the date they are laid so as to overcome the possibility of saving too long any eggs for hatching.

Some goose raisers think that it is best to wash goose eggs before setting them. This belief is based on the fact that when a goose makes her own nest and has access to water in which to swim she comes on the nest with her feathers wet. It is to simulate this condition that the eggs are washed. Certainly any dirty eggs should be washed.

Methods of Incubation. The most usual methods of hatching goose eggs are by means of the chicken hen and the goose. Incubators may also be used but do not as a rule seem to give as good results as they do with hen or duck eggs. Turkey hens may also be utilized for this purpose but are not commonly available although they make good mothers. Probably the most common method of hatching is the use of chicken hens. Next common is to allow the goose to hatch her own eggs. Goose eggs hatch well under hens or geese. During the height of the season nearly every fertile egg should hatch if the breeding geese are managed and fed so that they are in good condition. Early in the season the eggs may not run as fertile or hatch as well as later.

Period of Incubation. The period of incubation of goose eggs is approximately 30 days, but may vary from 28 to 33 or occasionally even 35 days.

Hatching with Chicken Hens. Chicken hens are used very commonly to hatch goose eggs both because they give good results and are readily available and also because it is desirable to take the first eggs laid by the geese away and not to let them get broody and sit so that they will lay more eggs. For the latter reason practically all the eggs laid early in the season are hatched by chicken hens.

The nest can be prepared for the hen either in a suitable place in a poultry house or in a shed or other building or in a box or barrel on the ground. As soon as the hen shows that she is ready to sit by staying on the nest, in which has been placed a nest egg or two, for a couple of nights in succession, she may be given a sitting of eggs. Four to 6 goose eggs will constitute a sitting for a common hen. The hen should be confined to the nest being let off only once a day for exercise, feed and water.

The sitting hen must be given good care, being even more particular in this respect than when she is sitting on hens' eggs as the period of incubation is longer. In addition to being careful to see that the hen comes off her nest for food and water she should be dusted 2 or 3 times during the hatch with some good insect powder to keep her free from lice and therefore contented to stay on the nest. Two or 3 days before the goslings hatch she should be dusted with especial care so that the goslings will be free from vermin.

On account of the large size of the eggs the hen should not be depended upon to turn them and this should be done by hand once or twice daily.

Hatching with Geese. All breeds of geese will hatch their eggs although some are more persistently broody than others while there is a considerable difference in individuals in this respect. Toulouse and Chinese are perhaps the least broody of the breeds and are sometimes termed non-broody. The eggs laid by geese are generally gathered as laid. If this were not done they will become broody and stop laying quicker than they do under this treatment.

The goose should be allowed to make her own nest. Often she will do this in a barrel, box or other shelter if these are conveniently available. When she shows that she is broody and has stopped laying she should be given a sitting of eggs which will consist of 10 or 11. Geese are often difficult to manage when they have young.

Wild and Egyptian geese should always be allowed to make their own nests which they like to do on dry ground near the water, using straw leaves or similar material to make the nest. They should not be disturbed as they are ugly during this time. They will hatch practically every egg.

Breaking Up Broody Geese. A goose which shows a desire to sit, can be broken up quite easily by confining her to a slat-bottomed coop without any feed, but with plenty of water to drink, for from 2 to 4 days. After being broken up she will generally commence laying again after an interval of a few days.

Hatching with an Incubator. While it is more difficult to hatch goose eggs in incubators than it is hen or duck eggs, this can be done by an experienced operator with a fair degree of success. The incubator should be operated at a temperature of 101.5 to 102.5 degrees F., with the thermometer so placed that the bulb is on a level with the top of the eggs. Beginning with the third day, the eggs should be turned twice a day as with hens' eggs. Beginning about the tenth day, the eggs should be cooled once a day, and they need more cooling than hens' eggs require. They should be cooled down to a temperature of about 80 to 85 degrees. All goose eggs whether in incubators or under hens or geese should be tested once during the hatch. The best time to do this is sometime between the tenth and fourteenth days, when any infertile eggs or dead germs should be thrown out.

Moisture for Hatching Eggs. Where eggs are being hatched in an incubator, there is need for the use of considerable moisture. It should be added first at about the end of the first week of incubation and should be repeated a couple of times during the second week. This can best be done by sprinkling the eggs liberally with water heated to about 100 degrees. Beginning with the 15th day and until 2 or 3 days before the eggs are ready to hatch soak them in warm water for from one-half a minute to a minute once every 2 or 3 days. For the last 2 or 3 days do this daily.

When the eggs are being hatched by chicken hens or geese in nests indoors or in boxes or barrels and in dry weather, moisture should be added in the same manner and with the same frequency and amount as in the incubator. When the nest is on damp ground, it is not necessary to use any moisture on the eggs.

Hatching. Goslings as a rule hatch rather slowly and somewhat unevenly, especially when under hens. For this reason it is well to remove each gosling as it hatches from under the hen or goose and place it in a covered, cloth-lined box or basket and keep near the stove until the hatch is completed. As soon as the hatch is over, the goslings that have been removed from the nest can be put back under the hen or goose which is to be allowed to assume the duties of motherhood.

CHAPTER XIII

Brooding and Rearing Goslings

When the hatch is completed all the goslings which have been removed from the nest should be returned; and the hen or goose removed to the coop which she is to occupy while brooding them. At this time, if hatched with a hen the goslings should be examined carefully on the head and neck to see whether there are any head lice present. If any are found the heads and necks of the goslings must be greased with a little lard or vaseline. Not too much grease should be used as it may prove harmful to the goslings.

Methods of Brooding. The most common methods of brooding goslings are the use of geese, of chicken hens or of artificial means. Geese make the best mothers but are not always available especially during the early hatches. Geese may also prove rather unruly when they have young and for this reason are not in favor with some goose raisers. When hatching is done simultaneously with geese and hens it is the practice of some raisers to give all the goslings hatched to the geese to rear.

Hens can be used very successfully for rearing goslings especially if they are confined to a coop for the first week or two so that they cannot range too far and too fast and tire the goslings out. Not over 6 or 8 goslings should be given to a hen to brood.

Artificial methods are very successful with goslings much more so in fact than are artificial methods of hatching the eggs. Some goose raisers prefer to use artificial means of brooding, especially if they have only a few goslings and are brooding at the same time some chicks or ducklings.

Brooding with Hens or Geese. A suitable roomy coop should be provided to which the goslings with their mother, either hen or goose, can be moved when the hatch is completed. The coop should be so constructed by means of a slatted front or otherwise, that the hen can be confined and the goslings allowed to range. It is very desirable to get the goslings out on grass as soon as possible. A goose with goslings is often allowed to have her liberty but many raisers prefer to confine her to a coop the same as when a hen is used. The coop should have a board floor well bedded with straw, shavings or similar material. This will not only help to keep the goslings dry but will also serve to protect them from their enemies during the night. For this same reason the coop should be so constructed that it can be closed at night by means of a wire covered door so as to shut out marauders, and at the same time allow plenty of ventilation. The coop must be cleaned often so as to keep the goslings clean and dry.

Length of Time Brooding Is Necessary. The time that goslings need brooding will, of course, depend upon the weather. During mild weather 10 days is usually sufficient, after which they can do without any brooding. Early in the season, brooding must be extended over a longer period. This may mean anywhere from 2 to 4 weeks or even longer.

Artificial Brooding. For this purpose any brooder utilized for chicks or ducks can be used for goslings. To start with they should have a temperature of about

100 degrees but this can be reduced in a few days until in a week or ten days it is only 70 to 80 degrees or if the weather is mild artificial heat may be dispensed with entirely. Where there are only a few goslings they may be put with a brood of ducks as long as they need heat. It does not work so well to put them with chicks both because they do not require a high temperature so long as the chicks and also because they are so large as to be likely to tread on and injure some of the chicks. Brooders should be well bedded with straw, shavings or some similar material and should be cleaned out every 2 or 3 days so as to be kept clean and dry. Do not crowd the goslings; give them plenty of room.

Some goose raisers do not depend upon heated brooders at all, especially when only a few goslings are to be brooded. For the first day or two the goslings are kept in a covered basket or box in the house near a fire and after this are put out during the warmth of the day but brought into the house and put in the basket or box at night until they are two or three weeks old. The same practice should be followed with goslings reared in brooders, these being used only during the night after the first 2 or 3 days, the goslings being put out-doors during the day in good weather.

When goslings which are being artificially brooded are put out during the day on the grass, they should be confined at first. This can be easily accomplished by building a triangular enclosure, formed of 3 boards, 1 foot wide or wider, placed up on edge. This enclosure can be easily shifted to a new position each day thus giving the goslings fresh ground and fresh grass.

General Care of Growing Goslings

Goslings should be kept dry and for this reason should be kept shut up until the dew is off the grass in the morning. For the same reason they should not be allowed access to water in which to swim until they are at least 3 or 4 weeks old. When allowed to swim, care should be taken to see that they can get out of the water easily.

Goslings caught in a cold rain will often be overcome and apparently dead. Frequently they can be revived and saved by wrapping them in a heated cloth and placing them near a warm fire. While they are still young, goslings should be driven under shelter whenever a rain storm comes up.

When allowed to run at liberty, goslings must be kept track of to some extent. They may become lost and have to be driven back to their shelter at night. Or they may fall into holes or get caught in fences and corners and must be released. When allowed to run with larger stock they are more or less liable to injury from being stepped upon or kicked.

A growing coop or shelter of some sort should be provided for the growing goslings although this is not always done after they are pretty well feathered out. Such a coop should be large enough so that the goslings are not crowded, and should be well ventilated. It should have a board floor and be capable of being closed so as to protect the goslings from their enemies, but without cutting off ventilation.

If natural shade is not available where the goslings range, artificial shade of some sort must be provided during the hot weather. Growing goslings are quite susceptible to extreme heat and will not make as good growth if not provided with shade. Artificial shade of boards or brush can be easily provided.

If for any reason it is necessary to confine growing goslings, they should be provided with good grass yards or runs and their coops or shelters should be moved to a fresh location frequently.

It is better, if possible, to keep the growing stock separate from the old breeding stock as they will do better and make more rapid growth under these conditions. Usually, however, where only a few geese are reared each year, old and young stock are allowed to range together.

Feeding the Goslings. Like chicks or ducks, goslings do not need to be fed as soon as hatched, the yolk of the eggs providing all the nourishment they need for at least 36 hours. They should, however, be furnished water to drink as soon as the hatch is completed.

The first feed should consist of stale bread, soaked in milk or water. With this material should be mixed boiled eggs chopped up fine. The goslings should be fed 3 or preferably 4 times daily until they are 2 or 3 weeks old. Chopped grass or some other green feed should be added to the feed, the quantity fed being increased steadily. It is important to get the goslings out on grass as soon as possible, which should be after the first 2 or 3 days if the weather is good, so that they will be able to graze for themselves. Five per cent of fine grit or sharp sand should likewise be added to the feed. Some growers prefer to feed the grit or sand in a hopper to which the goslings have constant access and from which they can help themselves. A constant supply of fresh drinking water is essential and this should be provided in drinking fountains or dishes such that the goslings cannot get their feet or bodies in them.

When a good grass range is available, the goslings, after they are 2 or 3 weeks old, will need only one light feed of mash daily in addition to the grass they eat. Such a mash will consist of 2 parts shorts and 1 part corn meal, ground oats or ground barley. Where the pasture is good many goslings are raised from the age of 2 or 3 weeks until they are ready to be fattened without any other feed than the grass and other material which they get for themselves. However, the feeding of one light feed of mash a day is advantageous as it insures adequate feed for their need and promotes quicker growth. After the goslings are 6 weeks old, if they are still fed, the mash should be changed to equal parts shorts, corn meal and ground oats with 5% meat scrap. This same mash can be continued until fattening time. Whole grains are not generally fed to goslings until they are well feathered and often not until it is desired to fatten them.

Percentage of Goslings Raised. Goslings are for the most part quite hardy and are comparatively easy to brood. This coupled with the fact that they are relatively free from disease and are not much troubled with insect pests makes it possible to raise a large per cent of the thrifty goslings hatched. With good care and with good strong healthy stock, it should be possible to raise in the neighborhood of 90% of the goslings hatched.

Rapidity of Growth. Goslings make a very rapid growth. When marketed as green geese they are usually turned off at from 12 to 16 weeks of age. At this age they should weigh from 9 to 12 pounds, depending upon the breed and upon the rapidity of growth. Many, probably most, young geese are not marketed at as early an age as this but are held until the Christmas season or later and marketed at heavier weight. The best grown Toulouse goslings should attain a weight of 16 to 18 pounds by Christmas or when 6 to 8 months old. Other breeds will weigh proportionately less. Special attention or special feeding will, of course, increase the weight over that attained without such feeding.

As a rule the heavier breeds such as the Toulouse do not get their full growth until they are about 18 months old. After this as geese of both sexes grow older, they will, of course, fill out more and attain greater weight.

Disease. Goslings are remarkably free from disease and a very large percentage of all strong goslings hatched should be reared. One of the principal difficulties is diarrhoea. This is usually caused by faulty feeding. It may be due to feeding too great a quantity of soft feed or to giving soft feed in too sloppy a condition. Access to stagnant water, unclean enclosures or unclean drinking dishes may also cause diarrhoea. When partly grown goslings which are being given soft feed are troubled with diarrhoea, this may sometimes be checked by substituting a light feed of corn daily for a part of the soft feed.

Goslings are sometimes troubled with lameness. This is usually caused by faulty feeding also, particularly by feeding a ration which is lacking in something needed, such as some form of animal feed like beef scrap which may cause a lack of mineral matter in the ration. If the goslings cannot secure it for themselves a supply of grit or gravel should be placed at their disposal.

There is an infectious disease of geese which sometimes causes trouble known as goose septicemia or hemorrhagic septicemia. This is a disease similar to fowl cholera and may attack either young or mature geese. It is not often found on farms where the geese are raised in small lots, but sometimes proves troublesome on farms where a large number of geese are gathered together for fattening. The geese are often found dead when one goes to feed them without having shown much preliminary sickness. The disease is usually fatal. Shortly before they die the affected geese may acquire an uncertain gait and may twist the head about and burrow it in the dirt. Treatment is of no avail. If the disease occurs in a flock, the affected birds should be removed and killed, while the rest of the flock should be moved to new ground if possible. The ground which they previously occupied should be plowed and any houses, shelter, feed troughs, and drinking vessels should be thoroughly disinfected.

CHAPTER XIV

Fattening and Marketing Geese

Classes of Geese Marketed. The market geese consist principally of the surplus young ganders not required for breeding purposes and such of the old geese of either sex as it may be considered desirable to get rid of. Some young females, when the number raised is in excess of the number required for breeders also find their way to market. While these geese are marketed in the largest numbers during the Thanksgiving and Christmas holiday season, particularly the latter, some geese of course find their way to market practically throughout the year. There is also a rather limited trade in "green geese" which corresponds to the trade in spring or "green" ducklings. Green geese are goslings about 12 to 16 weeks old, generally of the larger breeds, which are forced for rapid growth and are made to weigh in the neighborhood of 10 pounds at that age. These bring a good price and yield a good profit where there is demand for this class of geese.

Markets and Prices. As with most classes of poultry, the large cities offer the best market for geese. Especially the cities which have a large foreign population make good markets as many foreigners are more in the habit of using geese for a holiday dish than are native Americans. The most favorable market usually occurs at Christmas when roast goose and apple sauce is in considerable favor. Considerable numbers of geese are also used at Thanksgiving time and in recent years as the price of turkeys has steadily increased there has been an increasing tendency to substitute goose for turkey on that day. Following are prices paid for various classes of geese on the New York wholesale market from May 1920 to June 1921 as reported by the New York Produce Review. Quite a wide variation in price will be noted in many cases which reflects the difference in condition of the geese as received. In the case of express receipts of live geese where a wide variation in prices occurs the high quotations represent the receipt of especially fattened geese from nearby farms.

Prejudice Against Roast Goose. There exists on the part of some persons a prejudice against goose on the grounds that it is too greasy a dish. When improperly cooked, goose will prove to be too greasy to suit many fastidious palates but this condition is not so much the fault of the fowl as it is of the method of preparation and cooking. When dressed if the goose shows a large amount of abdominal fat, as it usually does and should, a large part of this should be removed. This fat when tried out is highly esteemed by many cooks and by other persons is treasured as an efficacious treatment for croup in children. Also while the goose is roasting, a part of the fat as it cooks out of the carcass should be removed. Treated in this way one need have no fear that the roast goose will prove too greasy but instead one will be pleasantly surprised at the rich taste which the roast goose possesses.

Methods of Fattening Geese for Market. Many geese are sent to market without any special treatment or effort to fatten them, being taken right off pasture in such condition as they happen to be or at best with only a half-hearted attempt to fatten them by feeding a little corn or some other grain for a short period. When a real effort is made to fatten geese for the market it is generally done in one of three ways. First is pen fattening which is the method best adapted to small lots of geese on the average farm. Second is by noodling which is only attempted in sections where the goose raisers are somewhat of specialists and where the effort is made to turn out geese of superior quality. Third is fattening in large flocks which is practiced only by a very limited number of farmers in scattered sections who take the unfattened geese raised on the general farms and finish them for market.

Pen Fattening. For this purpose the geese are put in pens large enough to hold them comfortably but without any yards. Not over 20 to 25 geese should be penned together for this purpose. To get the best results the geese should be kept as quiet as possible and to accomplish this the pens are partly darkened and the geese disturbed only at feeding time. The geese are fed three times daily; in the morning, at noon and at night, being given all they will clean up. One feed should consist of a moist mash composed of one part shorts and two parts corn meal. This mash should not be sloppy. The other two feeds consist mainly of corn with some oats or barley. Some roughage such as vegetables or hay should also be supplied. The pens should be deeply bedded with good oat straw. The geese will eat a considerable amount of this which thus helps to supply the roughage which they need. The straw also, of course, serves to keep the pen and the birds clean. A plentiful supply of good drinking water is also necessary. The usual period of fattening is three to five weeks and a gain of from 4 to 6 pounds per bird can be secured. This method of fattening is commonly used by goose raisers in Wisconsin and the geese from this state are noted for their fine quality.

A less intensive form of pen fattening is often used by farmers where a small yard is provided in addition to the pen itself and where no effort is made to darken the pen. If no other means for fattening are available, a small yard can be built, a few boards arranged for a shelter at one end and the birds fed in this enclosure as described above.

Noodling Geese. Noodling geese is a method of hand feeding which has for its purpose the production of the best fattened geese. It is not employed to any extent except in the section about Watertown, Wisconsin, where the farmers specialize to some extent on goose fattening. It is a method requiring long hours and tedious labor and cannot be profitably carried on unless a special price can be obtained for the product.

In noodling geese, 8 or 10 geese are placed in a pen about 8 by 12 feet which is heavily bedded with straw. A partition extends halfway across the pen and is utilized to keep the geese separate as they are fed. Young ganders and any old ganders or geese which are to be marketed are used for noodling.

The pen is kept dark and the geese should be disturbed only at feeding time. The first feed is given at 5 o'clock in the morning and five feeds are given daily at about 4 hour intervals, the last feed coming at 11 p. m. However, when the geese are first put on feed they are noodled only 3 times a day this being gradually increased to 5 times. The feeder sits on a box or stool in a corner of the pen, grasps each goose in turn holding it between his legs to keep it from struggling as he stuffs it with noodles. The goose is handled by its neck, never by its legs which are easily injured, and is held with its back toward the feeder. The feeder usually wears gloves to protect his hands from the severe bites which the birds will inflict. The feeder must also handle the birds as carefully as possible, especially as killing time approaches for the flesh bruises easily and the discolored patches spoil the appearance of the dressed goose.

The feeder at the start usually gives each goose from 3 to 5 noodles, gradually increasing this to 6 or 7 noodles if the birds will stand it, the number of noodles fed depending upon the size and condition of each bird, the feeder being obliged to use his judgment in this matter. In general if any feed can be felt in the craw, no noodles are given until the next feeding time. Failure to observe this is likely to cause the bird to go off feed. If any geese are noticed which are off feed they should be taken out and marketed.

The noodles are made of scalded corn meal, ground oats, ground barley and ground wheat or wheat flour, using equal parts of each. This material is thoroughly mixed and salted as one would bread and is then put through a sausage stuffer. The product as it comes from the stuffer is cut into noodles about 2?or 3 inches long and these are boiled for 10 or 15 minutes or until they float. A wash boiler with a wire rack forming a false bottom about 1?inches above the boiler bottom is used for this purpose. When cooked the noodles are dipped in cold water and then rolled in flour to keep them from sticking together. A supply of noodles is made which will last for 2 or 3 days' feeding.

Just before feeding, hot water is poured over the noodles to make them warm and slippery. The mouth of the goose is forced open and the noodles are put in, one at a time, and worked down by using the fingers on the outside of the neck. As each goose is fed it is placed on the other side of the partition until all in the pen have been fed. It is important that plenty of drinking water be kept before the geese.

The feeding period where geese are noodled usually extends from 3 to 4 weeks. Gains of 6 to 10 pounds per bird can be secured and often an increased price of 10 to 15 cents a pound can be secured for such specially fattened geese. Noodled geese will average about 25 pounds and some individuals have been made to weigh nearly 40 pounds. One man can noodle from 50 to 100 geese but has to put in long hours. Noodled geese should be dressed where fattened as they are soft fleshed and would shrink badly if shipped alive.

Fattening methods similar to the noodling described are used in parts of Europe for the production of the enlarged goose livers which are employed in making "patte de fois gras".

Methods Used on Fattening Farms

As previously mentioned, a few farmers make a specialty of buying the geese in their section of the country in the fall when it is too late for serious trouble to develop from hemorrhagic septicemia, a disease similar to fowl cholera, and to fatten or finish them in large flocks for the Thanksgiving and Christmas markets. Methods are employed in different sections which differ quite widely.

On a farm in the Middle West the geese are collected from the general farms where they are produced in small flocks and brought to the farm where they are kept in flocks as large as 1,000 or even more, and are allowed to run in a cornfield or orchard. They are fattened for about a month. Corn on the cob and plenty of water is kept before the geese all the time and if they are running in a cornfield they eat the leaves off the corn stalks for roughage. Roughage is supplied if not available otherwise and straw, hay or vegetables are utilized for this purpose.

No shelter is provided during mild weather, the geese getting such protection as they can from the trees or corn stalks. If the weather turns unusually severe, the geese are generally driven into sheds or barns. When fattened the geese are usually shipped to some large market alive. Several farms in the neighborhood of Boston make a specialty of finishing geese each fall, and the methods used are quite different from those described above. No geese are raised on these farms, the operation being confined to the fattening or finishing of the geese and to killing and dressing them for the market. Some of these goose fatteners also have stalls or stands in the Boston markets where they are enabled to dispose of their fattened geese to the best advantage.

[Illustration: FIG. 55. Large flock of geese fattening in an orchard. (Photograph from the Bureau of Animal Industry, U. S. Department of Agriculture.)]

Fatteners. In previous years these fatteners depended largely upon the geese produced on the Rhode Island farms for their supply. In the past few years, however, the supply from this source has dwindled greatly and the bulk of the geese for fattening are now shipped from Prince Edward Island, Canada, in carload lots. Such summer geese as are now fattened still come from Rhode Island and are brought in by truck. The fattening season begins in September and lasts until Christmas. Some early goslings are bought in June but there is not as good a profit from the summer geese, the demand and prices being adversely affected by the supply of spring ducklings available at that time.

Experience and good judgment will benefit the goose fattener greatly when purchasing his supply of geese for fattening. What he wants are goslings, not older geese, which have made a good growth and which have a large frame but which are in poor flesh rather than fat. Such geese will make more rapid and more profitable gains. When geese are bought for shipment by the carload from Prince Edward Island, they should be penned and fed at the point of shipment for 3 or 4 days before they are loaded in the cars, so as to put them in shape to stand the journey well. On the farms from which they come, the goslings are not fed much and in consequence are not in shape to stand shipment.

The Goslings which are secured from the farms for fattening are mainly common geese of no particular breed. Some pure bred geese are also obtained as are some first crosses between the pure breeds. A class of geese which is obtained in some numbers from Prince Edward Island and which is much desired is the so-called "Mongrel" goose. These are obtained by breeding a Wild or Canadian gander to geese of dark plumage similar to the Toulouse or African. The mongrel geese much resemble the wild gander in type and color and are in demand on the market because of their wild or gamy flavor. They bring about 10 cents per pound more than common geese. The market, however, is somewhat limited. These geese will not breed although the females will lay eggs. Where the wild gander is mated with light colored or white geese the offspring will have more or less light colored feathers and will not as closely resemble the wild parent and for this reason are not as desirable.

Shipping. The geese are loaded into stock cars into which three separate decks are built to accommodate them. From 1200 to 1400 geese can be loaded into a car thus arranged. The journey usually takes about 5 or 6 days and some fatteners send a man along with the car to feed and water the geese 2 or 3 times during the trip. If a man does not accompany the car, buckets of corn should be placed in the car for feed and some potatoes should also be supplied as these will serve in place of drinking water. If the car is not subjected to unusual delay, the geese should come through in good shape, but if much delayed there may be 25 to 100 geese dead when the car arrives at its destination.

When the car arrives at the end of its journey, the geese are unloaded and driven to the farm where they are turned into the fields together in a large flock. The fields in which they are thus kept should have a supply of growing green feed or grass and a good supply of fresh drinking water. They are kept here until they are wanted for the fattening pens which may be from a week to 20 days after their arrival at the farm. While in this large supply flock they are fed on corn and grass which they can get for themselves.

Summer Geese to be fattened are placed only about 50 in a pen or enclosure; and are provided with a few boards set on posts to protect them from the hot sun. The later geese are fattened in lots of 3 or 4 hundred or even more, depending upon how many pickers are available to be kept busy. It is for this reason also that the geese are not all put on the fattening ration at the same time, but are started at intervals so as to have a continuous supply coming along to keep the pickers busy. The geese not put in the fattening lots at the start are left in the fields to grow and develop until they are needed.

The enclosures in which the geese are penned for fattening are small lots or fields enclosed by stone walls or board fences 2?to 3 feet high. These lots should be dry and well-drained, a location on a side hill being good for this purpose. The fattening lots must be kept clean and stagnant water must not be allowed to stand in the lots as this is likely to cause sickness, especially diarrhoea. These yards should be plowed up each spring and planted to oats, corn or some other growing crop to sweeten them. No houses or shelters are provided for these geese but some yards are somewhat wooded which affords a measure of protection from the wind.

Feeding. When the geese are placed in the fattening lots, some fatteners prefer to fast the geese for from 3 to 5 days, giving them no feed but plenty of water to drink. This gives them a good appetite and puts them in good shape for fattening.

The geese are fed three times a day, in the morning, at noon and at night. The morning and night feed usually consists of a moist mixed feed fed in troughs; while the noon feed is whole corn thrown on the ground. The use of one feed of corn a day is supposed to check any tendency toward diarrhoea. In very cold weather some fatteners feed the mixed feed at noon and the corn at night. At first the geese are not given all they will eat but are worked up gradually, increasing the amount each day until they are getting all they want. As a rule the geese will drop back a little in feed consumption after they reach the point where they get all they want and from this time on, the feeding must be very carefully watched to see that they are not given so much that they will leave some to sour which would cause diarrhoea. The morning and noon feeds are lighter, the heaviest feed being given at night. The bird's appetites will vary from day to day so that it is best to make the rounds twice in feeding to make sure that they have enough and that none is left. If any is left it must be gathered up and carried away.

No provision is made for furnishing the fattening geese with green feed or roughage. The practice with respect to drinking water varies. Some fatteners keep a supply before the birds in troughs which must be washed out each day to keep them clean. Others furnish no water except that used in mixing up the feed.

Corn Meal is the principal ingredient of the fattening mixture. To a sack of corn meal is added 10% beef scrap and five good shovels of grit or medium sized gravel. In addition some fatteners add 10% of flour to bind the mixture together. This material should be thoroughly mixed up in a dry state as a better mix can be obtained in this way. It is then mixed up with water, the practice here varying. Some fatteners mix in a trough with boiling water a short time before feeding, while others mix it with cold water letting it soak over night and adding more water in the morning if it is too dry at that time. It should be mixed until it can be shoveled readily but should be quite solid, never in a sloppy condition as this is likely to cause diarrhoea. A little salt may be added, if desired, as an appetizer. While corn meal is generally used, hominy may take its place. After the geese are started on the fattening ration, this must be given throughout the fattening period. Changing to some other feed will throw the geese off feed and cause a loss.

Feeding. When the mixed feed is ready it is shoveled into boxes or barrels on a low wagon and driven to the fattening lots where it is shoveled into the troughs for the geese. Ordinary V-shaped troughs are favored instead of flat troughs as the latter afford hiding places for rats which may cause damage in addition to the feed which they eat by frightening the geese.

Geese are easily frightened and must therefore be handled rather carefully and gently as a severe fright will interfere with the gains they will make. Some fatteners provide electric lights where the geese rest at night so that they can see and will not be so likely to become frightened.

When the geese are ready to be killed they are driven up to the killing house and into a pen where they may be easily caught. Each goose as caught is examined to see whether it is in condition for killing. If it is not it is put back with a later lot for additional fattening. Good condition in a goose is judged by its weight when handled and also by the condition of its breast and the fat on its back. A good place to test geese for fat is on the side of the body just below the point where the wing joins the body. If fat can be seized between the thumb and finger at that point, the goose is in good condition.

Dry Picking. All fattened geese for the Boston market are dry picked. The goose is held between the knees of the picker with the wings held fast against the sides of the body. The head is grasped by the left hand, the mouth forced open and the veins in the back of the throat just beyond the skull severed with a sharp knife for the purpose of bleeding the bird. If the bird is to be stuck, which is not always done, the point of the knife is then plunged through the roof of the mouth to the brain. The legs are then seized in the left hand, together with the ends of the wings to prevent the goose from struggling and the goose is struck once or twice sharply on the back of the head with a club held in the right hand. This is for the purpose of stunning the bird. The geese may also be bled by sticking the knife through the neck from the outside just below the head.

The picker then takes his seat beside the feather box, holding the goose on his lap with the head held between his knee and the outside of the box. He proceeds to pluck the feathers as rapidly as possible, removing all the feathers except the main wing feathers or those of the first joint of the wing and the feathers of the neck half way from the head to the body. All the soft body feathers are thrown in the box and saved. The coarser feathers are thrown on the floor. The down is removed by rubbing the moistened hand over the skin. To save the hands, ordinary rubber heels dipped in water are often used. Sharp knives are also used to shave off the pin feathers which cannot be plucked and any down not removed by rubbing.

The dry picked goose presents a much better appearance than a scalded goose and the feathers are more valuable. The skin of a dry picked bird is not so likely to be rubbed off in removing the down.

The Value of the Feathers is sufficient to pay for the cost of the picking or perhaps a little more. The cost of picking in the fall of 1920 ranged from 15 to 20 cents per goose where the picker was boarded and 24 cents without board.

A good man can pick about 40 geese in a day. Women are not employed for this work as the geese are too big and too strong for them to handle.

After the geese are picked, the blood is washed from the head and the feet washed if that is necessary. They are then thrown into barrels of cold water to cool and must be left there until the body heat is entirely removed. The wings are tied in place by means of a string or tape tied around the body and wings and the legs may also be crossed over the back and tied. The geese when ready for market are either shipped in by express or are taken in by automobile truck.

Gain in Weight. In fattening according to the methods described above a gain in weight is secured of from 6 to 8 pounds per goose. This does not represent the total gain in value, however, for the fattened geese will bring more per pound as a result of their finished condition. The fattened geese when ready for market will weigh from 12 to 20 pounds. Weights taken on two carloads of fattened geese showed an average weight of 14 pounds. On December 2, 1920, fattened geese from these farms were bringing 42 cents per pound on the Boston market while the mongrel geese were worth 50 cents or a little better.

The question may arise as to the size of farm necessary to carry on a business of this sort. Using the methods employed about Boston a farm of 30 acres would be sufficient to handle 20,000 geese in a season. In selecting a farm for such a purpose, a location should be chosen where there are no close neighbors as the odor from the geese and yards is offensive to most persons.

Selling Geese Alive. Most farmers who raise only a few geese ship them alive, either sending them to some commission house or selling them to someone who makes a specialty of fattening. Such geese are often in poor condition and bring the lowest quotation. Large coops similar to those used for turkeys should be used in shipping geese.

Killing. Where geese are killed on the farm for shipment to market they are usually hung up by means of a cord about the legs. When geese are to be dry picked the veins in the throat just beyond the skull are first severed with a long bladed knife such as used for killing turkeys to cause good bleeding and the point of the knife is then plunged through the roof of the mouth to the brain performing the stick which serves to make the feathers come out more easily as with other classes of poultry. Since it is rather difficult to dry pick geese, they are usually scalded or steamed and where this is done, the stick is not made but after the veins in the throat are cut, the goose is stunned by a blow on the back of the head with a short club. A blood can or weight is then hooked through the lower bill which keeps the neck straightened out and prevents the blood from being thrown about the room or on the birds. The birds are allowed to hang until they are dead and thoroughly bled out.

Picking. When geese are dry picked, the feathers are removed just as soon as the birds are stuck for the longer the delay the harder the feathers pull. The wings are picked to the first joint and the feathers of the neck half-way to the head. The soft pin feathers and fine down may be removed by shaving the skin or rubbing the body with moistened hands will partially remove them.

Usually geese are scalded or steamed for picking. For steaming a wash boiler three-quarters full of boiling water and with a burlap sack tightly stretched over its top can be used. The goose is simply laid on the sack and the steam coming through the burlap steams the feathers and makes them easy to remove. The breast should be steamed first, then the back and then each side. Two or three minutes will be time enough to complete the steaming. The feathers are steamed until they pull out easily. The goose must be kept moving to prevent the flesh from becoming scalded and since the breast is especially tender it is usual to lay the head under the breast to prevent the latter from scalding. After steaming the body feathers are removed and the bird is then singed over a flame furnished by alcohol burned in shallow tin plates, in order to remove the down. The down may also be removed by sprinkling powdered rosin over the goose's body which is then dipped into hot water. The hot water melts the rosin which sticks to the down and the down and rosin can then be rubbed off together.

Geese may also be steamed by scalding slightly in hot water and then wrapping tightly in burlap or some other cloth. They are kept wrapped for about five minutes which allows the steam to work thoroughly through the feathers which can then be plucked easily.

Exactly the same methods can and often are employed in dressing geese as are used with ducks. The reader is therefore also referred to the material in Chapter VII.

There seems to be no great insistence on the part of most markets for dry picked geese. Some will pay slightly more for the dry picked birds but others make no difference.

Packing for Shipment. After picking, the geese are washed and then placed in cold water to cool. Ice water is best for this purpose and is essential in warm weather. The carcasses must be allowed to remain in the water until they are thoroughly cooled, which will take at least one to two hours. If any animal heat is left in the bodies, they will spoil very quickly. Often the carcasses are dipped in hot water, before being thrown in the cold water, to plump them. After they are thoroughly cooled, the geese are packed in barrels for shipping. If the weather is cool they may be packed in well ventilated barrels without ice, but if the weather is warm, cracked ice must be used in packing, proceeding in the same way as when packing ducks as described on page 109. It is always risky to pack without ice.

Saving the Feathers. Goose feathers are valuable and should therefore be saved when the geese are plucked. The soft body feathers and the coarser feathers should be kept separate. The feathers should be cured by spreading them out in a thin layer on the floor of a loft or room, stirring them up occasionally until they are thoroughly dried out, when they can be sacked and sold. Failure to dry the feathers thoroughly will result in their heating and molding with the result that they will arrive at their destination in bad shape and will be worth less money. The soft body feathers of geese are practically all used in making beds and pillows while the quills are sometimes utilized in making toothpicks and cigarette holders. Prices for goose feathers in June 1921 were as follows:

Pure White dry picked 75c per lb. Good average white " " 65c " " Largely gray " " 55c " " Largely gray scalded 40c " " Long goose quills 5c " "

These prices were for good dry feathers.

Plucking Live Geese for their Feathers

In the days of feather beds and home-made pillows the practice of plucking live geese for their feathers was very common. Now, however, with the demand for goose feathers less and with the opinion of some breeders that plucking geese is both cruel and injurious, the practice seems to be decreasing. Many goose raisers in the South and a less number in the Middle West and North however still pluck the feathers from the live geese prior to the time of moulting. The frequency with which the picking is done varies greatly, some picking as often as every six weeks during the spring, summer and early fall while others pick twice, once in the spring and once in the fall, or once in the spring only. Geese should never be picked during the late fall or winter when the weather is cold or during the breeding season. Both young and old geese are plucked and the average yearly production of feathers per goose is about one pound. When the quills of the feathers are dry and do not contain any blood, the feathers are ripe for picking. In plucking, a stocking is placed over the head of the goose and the goose held on the lap and between the legs during the process.

An assistant to hold the goose during the plucking simplifies the work greatly. In plucking, part of the soft feathers of the breast, sides, abdomen and back are taken but these sections should not be plucked clean. It is especially important that enough short feathers be left to support the wings.

After plucking, the feathers must be cured before they are shipped. This may be done by spreading them out on a floor as described for the feathers taken from slaughtered geese or they may be placed loosely in burlap sacks and hung up in a garret or loft. Hanging in this way and in the loosely woven sacks, they are subjected to a good circulation of air and will dry out without heating. Sacks of feathers should not be piled or packed closely together, on top of one another or even be allowed to lie on the floor until they are thoroughly dry as otherwise they are almost sure to heat and mold.

Transcriber's Notes

Apart from minor changes to formatting, table alignment and punctuation, the only changes made to the text from the original are as follows:

Preface (2nd page): "minumum" changed to "minimum" (... with the minimum of initial investment and of labor.)

"Sebastapool" changed to "Sebastapol" in List of Illustrations (Egyptian

Gander and Sebastapol Goose) Figure 50 caption, and twice in the index. This is consistent with the use of "Sebastapol" in the text.

Page 20: "neccessary" changed to "necessary" (... it becomes neccessary to mate a smaller number of females ...).

Page 30: missing page reference added (See Page 14).

Page 72: comma deleted after "Of" (Of course, eggs sufficient to fill the entire incubator capacity ...).

Fig 28 caption: "yords" changed to "yards" (Long brooder house and yards with feeding track.)

Page 107: duplicate word "the" deleted (... hung in a steam box with the heads outside ...)

Page 131: "chickens" changed to "chicken" (Ducklings can be brooded if desired by means of chicken hens.)

Page 136: missing page reference added (... in accordance with the directions given on page 106).

Page 137: missing page reference added (See page 119).

Page 141: "1920" changed to "1910" (The census figures of 1920 compared with those for 1910 ...)

Page 145: "in" changed to "is" (An objection to geese often expressed but without good foundation is that they will spoil the pasture for other stock.)

Page 154: "Ameriacn" changed to "American" (... the American Standard of Perfection.)

Page 155 Footnote: "standard" changed to initial upper case "Standard" (American Standard of Perfection).

Page 163: missing page reference added (The same method of packing the eggs should be employed as with duck eggs described on page 137.)

Page 165: "thoughout" changed to "throughout" (... green feed available throughout the summer and fall ...)

Page 166: "penus" changed to "penis" (... the penis will protrude.)

Page 182: "close" changed to "closed" (It should have a board floor and be capable of being closed ...)

Page 194: "pleasanty" changed to "pleasantly" (...one will be pleasantly surprised at the rich taste which the roast goose possesses.)

Page 211: missing page reference added (... in the same way as when packing ducks as described on page 109.)

Page 222 (Index): "stipling" changed to "stippling" (Gray stippling on Penciled Runner drakes).

Made in the USA
Las Vegas, NV
15 November 2021

34467039R00069